CARIBBEAN
ISLANDS

JPMGUIDES

CONTENTS

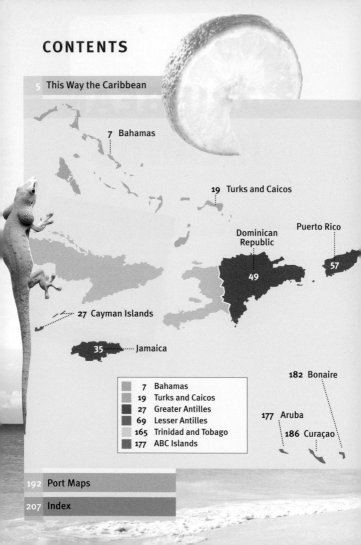

5 This Way the Caribbean

7 Bahamas

19 Turks and Caicos

Dominican Republic **49**

Puerto Rico **57**

27 Cayman Islands

35 Jamaica

182 Bonaire

177 Aruba

186 Curaçao

7	Bahamas
19	Turks and Caicos
27	Greater Antilles
69	Lesser Antilles
165	Trinidad and Tobago
177	ABC Islands

192 Port Maps

207 Index

75	US Virgin Islands
69	British Virgin Islands
97	Anguilla
86	Sint Maarten
106	Saint-Martin
109	Saint-Barthélemy
101	Antigua and Barbuda
96	Montserrat
86	Saba Statia
127	St Kitts and Nevis
111	Guadeloupe
132	Dominica
119	Martinique
138	St Lucia
144	Barbados
150	St Vincent and the Grenadines
158	Grenada
165	Trinidad and Tobago

Port Maps

192	Nassau
194	Montego Bay
195	La Romana
196	Santo Domingo Old Town
197	Old San Juan
198	Pointe-à-Pitre
199	Philipsburg
200	Fort-de-France
201	Saint John's
202	Roseau
203	Bridgetown
204	Kingstown
205	Saint George's
206	Willemstad

Fold-out map
Caribbean Islands
Jamaica
Puerto Rico

Traditional dancers bring a smile to the Dominican Republic.

THIS WAY THE CARIBBEAN

The Caribbean islands stretch between North and South America; in the west the Greater Antilles are comprised of four solo islands as well as the paradisical Cayman Islands. To the east, the Lesser Antilles form a rainbow arching from north to south. The alluring archipelago of the Bahamas spreads extensively to the northwest of the diver's heaven which is Turks and Caicos. The ABC Islands are situated to the east of the contrary Trinidad and Tobago.

Islands of Plenty

Specks of emerald set in a turquoise sea, beaches of fine white or golden sand fringed by shady palms swaying gently in the breeze, a colourful, luxuriant vegetation—the islands provide the perfect answer to our longing for escape, for peace and serenity and eternal sunshine.

But history has not been kind to the region. Fabulous myths of Indian tribes and cannibals mingle with disappointed hopes of an El Dorado or a Fountain of Youth. Pirates and buccaneers ruled the waves. The Spaniards came and conquered, soon to be supplanted by the English and their bitter rivals, the French. Then Dutch, the Danes and the Swedes sallied forth in search of Antilles pearls to fasten to their royal crowns. The deeds and mis-deeds of European rule gave rise to the differences in the islands, some of them rich, some poor, each one unique.

From Sugar to Soca

The majority of today's islanders are descendants of slaves. Having exhaused the Amerindian inhabitants, European settlers turned to Africa for the massive workforce required for the cultivation of sugar, the white gold of the 18th century. If the wounds of past tragedy have not quite healed, the blending of peoples has resulted, with time, in a new cultural identity, original and full of optimism. With a colourful language and tropical good humour, the Creole soul pulses rhythmically, finding its utmost expression in reggae or soca music and carnival—and a welcoming glass of rum punch.

A magical moment as the sun dips towards the horizon.

BAHAMAS

Strewn over a vast expanse of the Atlantic Ocean, the Bahamas bask in breezy semi-tropical sunshine. Starting as close as 80 km (50 miles) to the Florida coast, the archipelago swoops southeast for some 1,000 (600 miles) almost to Haiti and eastern Cuba. Of the 700-odd islands, only around 20 are at least minimally inhabited, and a few dozen have vacation facilities. Another 2,000 smaller cays (pronounced "keys") are blissfully deserted.

New Providence

The main population centres are Freeport on Grand Bahama Island and Nassau, capital of the Commonwealth of the Bahamas, on New Providence Island.

Nassau

With its glitter and sophistication, its daytime traffic jams and night-time entertainment, Nassau (population 256,000) is certainly not typical of the Bahamas. But it's definitely a magnet for tourists. Huge cruise ships discharge their passengers on the Prince George Wharf, just opposite the historic centre. On the wharf, pop into the Junkanoo Expo, a small museum showcasing the brilliant costumes and floats from the famous parade held on December 26 and New Year's Day.

City Centre

Facing Rawson Square, the pink picture-postcard **Public Buildings** dating from 1812 and a marble statue of Queen Victoria (1905) recall the British colonial era. Behind the Parliament and the Court House, the town's oldest building is the **Public Library** (1797). The octagonal construction was originally a prison. Its museum displays old prints, maps and portraits, a carved stone Arawak ceremonial stool and other artefacts.

The commercial centre of the city, **Bay Street**, stretches westwards from Rawson Square to the **Straw Market** at Market Plaza. The amiable sales ladies here have been creating straw items since childhood. Next to the market, the historic Vendue House is home to the **Pompey Museum**. Devoted to the history of slavery in the West

BAHAMAS FLASHBACK

Early times
The islands are inhabited from the 4th century. Arawak Indians from Lucaya settle on the archipelago in the 9th or 10th centuries.

15th–16th centuries
Christopher Columbus lands at an island he names San Salvador on October 12, 1492. Unsuccessful in his search for gold and other riches, he sails out of the Bahamas towards neighbouring Cuba. The Spanish deport the Indian inhabitants of Lucaya on Grand Bahama Island to work in Spain, Haiti and Cuba.

17th century
A group of English Puritans from Bermuda establish the first permanent European settlement on Eleuthera in 1648, followed in 1666 by a second colony on New Providence Island. Charles II of England grants the Bahamas to six Lords Proprietors, who are powerless to suppress the piracy that rages in the archipelago. Blackbeard, Henry Morgan and other corsairs operate out of Nassau.

18th–19th centuries
The Bahamas become a crown colony in 1718. The first royal governor cleans out the pirates and calls an Assembly. English Loyalists fleeing the American War of Independence settle in the islands. The population trebles in a few years, thanks in part to the slaves brought here by their Confederate masters. Cotton plantations flourish but prosperity is short-lived. The weak soil is soon depleted and a plague destroys crops. Most planters leave the islands. Nassau becomes a free port in 1787. Slavery, never widespread, is officially abolished in 1833.

20th century–present
Massive emigration takes place, mainly to the United States. During Prohibition, Nassau booms as a centre for bootlegging. The city's first gambling casino opens in 1920, and an air service links Nassau to Miami nine years later. An offshore banking boom begins in the 1930s. During World War II American bases are established in the Bahamas and the Duke of Windsor becomes governor. Tourism increases steadily, especially after the Cuban revolution. The Bahamas achieve self-government and, in 1973, independence, but retain membership of the Commonwealth. The first black governor-general, Sir Milo Butler, is appointed after independence. The economy prospers from tourism and offshore finance.

Indies and Bahamas, the museum is named after a slave who raised a rebellion at the Rolle plantation on Exuma island.

Follow George Street to the Anglican **Christ Church Cathedral** (1841), built from local limestone in an airy Gothic style. At the corner of George Street and King Street, the **Pirates of Nassau** attraction gives an interactive account of buccaneering days.

At the top of George Street, overlooking downtown Nassau, the pink-painted Neoclassical **Government House** was the residence of governors and governor-generals for more than 200 years. It is closed to the public but you can walk up to the statue of **Columbus** and take photos of the guards, or just enjoy the bay views.

On Market Street, parallel to George Street, **Balcony House** is one of the oldest wooden buildings in town; dating from the second half of the 18th century, it is furnished in period style.

West Hill Street, west of Government House, takes you to the **National Art Gallery** in a superb colonial mansion of 1860. Works by renowned local artists are enhanced by temporary exhibitions.

Opposite the post office on Parliament Street, look out for **Jacaranda House**, a lovely old building constructed with stones brought as ballast on a ship in 1840. The house is used for cultural events.

istockphoto.com/NaluPhoto

Swimming with the dolphins is the experience of a lifetime.

Slaves hacked the 66 steps of the **Queen's Staircase** in Elizabeth Avenue from the black rock cliff as a passageway for troops garrisoned above at **Fort Fincastle**. At the top, you'll reach Nassau's water tower, which offers a stunning panorama of the harbour and Paradise Island.

Beneath the toll bridge over to Paradise Island, **Potters Cay** is a fun little spot: fishing boats tie up at the waterside, their catch of conch, grouper and snapper cooked up into local specialities at a row of low-key shacks.

Paradise Island

"Welcome to Paradise" says the sign just after you've paid your bridge toll and made the 5-minute crossing to the island on foot. Pearly gates there aren't, but you immediately see tall casuarina trees and palms, which cover much of this charming resort. You can also get here via a water taxi from Rawson Square.

For centuries the tiny sliver of an islet was uninhabited, but in recent years it has been developed into a complete "destination within a destination". It is largely taken up by **Atlantis Paradise Island**, a huge modern resort dreamed up by South African hotel magnate Sol Kerzner. It combines some of the world's most expensive hotel accommodation with casino, shopping mall, aquarium, water parks, golf, fitness centre, speedway and a marina. You can swim with the dolphins and hand-feed stingrays at the Water's Edge lagoon.

The rest of the island has residential districts, extensive facilities for golf and other sports, and a marina called **Hurricane Hole**, where the yacht-watching can be eyebrow-raising. Of the excellent beaches strung out along the island's north shore, **Paradise Beach** is the best known, but **Cabbage Beach** is just as beautiful.

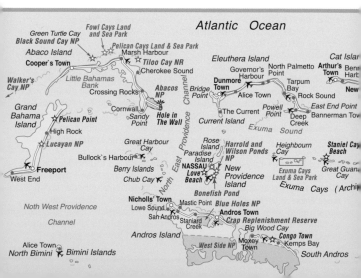

Toward the eastern end of the island are the **Versailles Gardens**, with statuary adorning a row of manicured terraces—the gazebo here is a favourite locale for weddings—and its **French Cloister**. Originally built in the 14th century by Augustinian monks in Montréjeau near Lourdes, France, the cloister was shipped here in pieces in the 1920s by newspaper magnate William Randolph Hearst. It was assembled in the 1960s.

A popular excursion goes to **Blue Lagoon Island** (Salt Cay) where you can swim with dolphins and sea lions and enjoy the crystal clear waters of a natural lagoon as well as many white-sand beaches.

West of the Centre

The British-built **Fort Charlotte**, located on a hill above **Clifford Park**, is awash with colonial history.

West of Nassau, the **Ardastra Gardens, Zoo & Conservation Centre** are renowned for the marching flamingos, Bahama parrots, rock iguanas and native boa constrictors. Further west is the **Cable Beach** resort area, where amusements abound.

At the western tip of New Providence Island, the **Clifton Heritage National Park** preserves local history in its colonial-era ruins and a staircase carved into the cliff by pirates. There are also splendid beaches, trails and eco-tours.

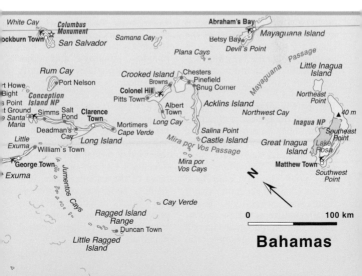

Grand Bahama

Some 90 km (56 miles) from the coast of Florida lies the appealing island of Grand Bahama. Freeport/Lucaya, its major centre, is located on the south-west coast.

Freeport

This commercial and resort centre is even less typical of the Bahamas than Nassau. Despite English place names and tours by red London double-decker bus, basic Bahamian local colour is in short supply here. The atmosphere is more palpably American than anywhere else in the Commonwealth. Not unexpectedly, since it was a Virginia financier, Wallace Groves, who conceived the "Freeport miracle" and set it in motion in 1955. Most of the island's residents live in Freeport—or at the West End settlement 40 km (25 miles) away.

Lucaya

The sprawling **Lucaya** resort area, just east of Freeport, features beachfront and marina hotels and the island's best golf courses. The huge **Port Lucaya Marketplace**, combining shops, restaurants and bars, notably around Count Basie Square, is one of Freeport's major sightseeing attractions. Every evening a different show or concert is held on the square named after the famous jazzman who spent several years on the island. North of the Marketplace, the **Perfume Factory** produces lovely fragrances from local ingredients such as jasmine, ginger and spices. You can watch scents being blended and create your own perfume.

To the north, on East Settlers Way, the **Rand Nature Centre** offers self-guided walks (with an info map) and guided tours through 100 acres of protected Bahamian forest dotted with interpretive boards. You can photograph parrots and other birds, and spot 21 varieties of orchid. The visitor centre offers information on local fauna and flora alongside Lucayan Indian artefacts.

From Bell Channel Bay, wind conditions permitting, **glass-bottom boats** take tourists over coral gardens and along Grand Bahama's deep reef. Sharks, barracudas, stingrays and other intriguing creatures can usually be spotted.

The Underwater Explorers Society (UNEXSO) organizes a unique attraction, the **Dolphin Experience**, enabling you to encounter and swim with dolphins. Four times a day, a boat leaves for the Sanctuary Lagoon on the south coast of the island. There, in a shallow pool, you can observe and touch the dolphins; specialists provide information on these friendly and intelligent marine mammals.

DINING AND SHOPPING

On the menu

Island chefs specialize in some interesting seafood variations, many of which contain conch. This chewy mollusc is prepared in a multitude of ways: fried; stewed; in soup (chowder); and in salad (with onions, celery, peppers and tomatoes). Grouper, a flaky white fish, is the most popular in the Bahamas, but don't pass by red snapper in anchovy sauce either. Spiny lobster and crab come in many guises: steamed, creamed, minced, grilled, baked, stewed, devilled or stuffed. Peas'n'rice is a popular accompaniment.

For dessert try guava duff—a pie made from the local aromatic guava fruit, served with rum sauce.

Rum figures in a whole gamut of tropical drinks. Have it in piña colada (with coconut cream and pineapple juice), Yellow Bird (with coffee, banana liqueur and fruit juices) or Skinny Minnie (with Galliano, cream, Cointreau coconut liqueur and grenadine), to name but a few.

The local liqueur is Nassau Royal, good by itself or in coffee.

Leading American soft drinks are sold everywhere, but for a refreshing change try canned sea-grape soda.

The best buys

Coconut-shell artefacts and jewellery are said to be nearly indestructible. Conch and whelk shells or sharks' teeth may also be used for jewellery. Printed fabrics, particularly batiks from Andros, are hand-waxed and dyed. Straw goods take in everything from sunhats and carry-alls to models of Nassau surrey horses. Woodcarvings are also popular. Rum is a firm favourite, especially Eleuthera pineapple rum and the coconut variety.

Freeport/Lucaya offers a wide range of tax-exempt goods at affordable prices in its bonded area: china, porcelain, cutlery, fabrics, glass, leather, perfumes, silver, watches, cameras and alcohol.

Philip H. Koblenz

"Please do not touch the plants —many are poisonous", says the sign at the **Garden of the Groves**. That's the only jarring note in these delightful 4.5 ha (11 acres) of tropical flora, man-made waterfalls and ponds. Lizards dart by as you stroll among the 10,000 plants and trees, and a multitude of birds make the gardens their home. You can also explore a labyrinth and a replica of the gardens' original chapel.

West of Freeport

To the west of Freeport is a string of closely touching settlements collectively known as **Eight Mile Rock**. Several ancient cannonballs have been found in this area in recent times, though not even pirates were supposed to have lived on Grand Bahama until the 1840s.

Signs make good reading along the road, as you pass such places as **Sea Grape**, **Deadman's Reef** (said to be the best diving spot) and **Bottle Bay**.

West End, sadly, isn't the roguish place it used to be. Searching the sleepy seaside village, you'll find only the scantiest traces of the bad old days of prohibition when merchants and rum runners made their fortunes here, smuggling liquor into the "dry" United States. From here you can go on deep-sea fishing and scuba-diving excursions.

East of Freeport

If your time is not limited, visit the **Lucayan National Park** some 30 km (18.6 miles) east of Freeport, with its natural forest, mangrove swamp and limestone caves, two of which are open to the public.

On a trip to this end of the island you travel alongside the majority of Grand Bahama's advertised 100 km (60 miles) of beaches, mostly long, windswept stretches of sand frequented only by birds and crabs. **Pelican Point** is a tidy, friendly roadside settlement where the centre of all things is the Baptist church.

Tiny **McLean's Town**, with its clutch of pastel wooden houses, is unusual in that the town's women (as well as its men) earn their living from fishing. Locals will be happy to tell you about the annual Conch Cracking Competition on Discovery Day, October 12, when great crowds turn up to watch contestants crack, empty and clean up to 25 conches in less than three minutes.

At a fishing resort on nearby **Deep Water Cay**, there's great bonefishing in the shallows among the east end mangroves, and shelling can be superb along **Crabbing Bay** and **John Davis** beaches.

Air-conditioned local buses stop at many top sights, and a 1-week Bahamas Get-A-Round pass (www.viator.com) gives unlimited travel on them.

Out Islands

The islands and cays "out and away" from the hubs of Nassau and Freeport are called the Out Islands (or sometimes the Family Islands). These are some of the most popular ones.

The Abacos

Many of the cays in this archipelago north of New Providence were founded by Loyalists from New England and the Carolinas at the time of the American Revolution, and a number of the towns still have something of a New England air about them.

A 200-year-old tradition of shipbuilding is still in evidence in **Man-O-War Cay**. The town is the home of the Abaco dinghy, the sturdy little sailboat that was the work boat of the Bahamian fishermen and traders for two centuries. You're invited to watch as carpenters meticulously handcraft each boat.

Green Turtle Cay is the site of one of the oldest settlements on the outer cays. The village of **New Plymouth** was founded by Loyalists in 1783. Today it still looks much like it did in the 18th century: a small New England fishing village. Flower-bordered lanes lead past clapboard houses decorated in "gingerbread" style. Landmarks include the old colonial jail, a 200-year-old cemetery, the 150-year-old Commissioner's Office and the **Albert Lowe Memorial Museum**, with an outstanding collection of colonial artefacts. A must-see is a local tavern, Miss Emily's Blue Bee Bar, where you can sample Goombay Smash cocktail, made with local rum and fruit juice.

The Abacos have some of the best diving and snorkelling sites in the Bahamas, notably in **Pelican Cays Land and Sea Park**, a 850 ha (2,100 acre) underwater preserve with possibilities for night dives.

Marsh Harbour on Great Abaco Island is the bare-boat charter centre of the northern Bahamas. At nearby Hope Town, if you're feeling energetic, climb the 100 steps of the pink and white candy-striped lighthouse for a picturesque view.

Treasure Cay has more leisure facilities, including an 18-hole championship golf course and tennis courts.

Eleuthera

Outstanding tourist amenities abound in this "garden island" rich in pineapple plantations, and endowed with beautiful beaches and fantastic dive sites. It was settled by Puritan pilgrims from Bermuda in 1648 and they gave it the name which is Greek for "Freedom". One mile off the northern coast, accessible by water ferry, lies the pretty **Harbour Island**, famous for its sheltered pink beach and the beautiful village of **Dunmore Town**. The original capital of the Bahamas, it is a photographer's dream.

Cat Island

Wide beaches, deep creeks, pre-Columbian Arawak Indian caves, and fertile, scenic hills are the attractions here. On the highest "peak", 63 m high, stands the monastery of **Mount Alvernia**, once home of a hermit-monk Father Jerome.

San Salvador

The contested site of Columbus's first landing in the New World, San Salvador is another favourite for scuba diving and game fishing.

Long Island

Sharing the coastline with rugged cliffs are scores of dazzling white sand beaches. More than 30 shipwrecks can be explored off nearby **Conception Island**.

Exumas

Yachtsmen love to cruise this long string of mostly uninhabited isles and cays. Several large resorts are clustered around **Elizabeth Harbour** on Great Exuma. Inland are some poignant ruins of once-great plantation houses.

Andros

This island's reef is a scuba and snorkel wonderland. Beyond the reef, the ocean bottom descends rapidly to a depth of 8 km (5 miles)—called the "Tongue of the Ocean"—fabulous for fishing.

Bimini

Ernest Hemingway brought the island a certain fame when he resided in Alice Town, in Blue Marlin Cottage. The **Bimini Museum** has mementos of his stay alongside local history displays.

Berry Islands

Its 30 cays amount to a total of only about 30 sq km (11 sq miles), but there are some chic resort facilities as well as cavern, reef and wreck dive sites. Boaters also find much to revel in here, as do golfers (at **Great Harbour Cay**) and beach connoisseurs.

Crooked Island

Quaint villages cluster along the creeks and tidal flats. Yours may be the only footprints on the magnificent beaches of this bonefishing paradise.

Great Inagua

The southernmost and third largest island in the Bahamas is known for its important salt production and **Lake Windsor**, part of the Inagua National Park, where flamingos come to mate each spring. Tours can be arranged through the Bahamas National Trust in Nassau.

THE HARD FACTS

Climate. The Bahamas are blessed with a mild subtropical climate. During the summer months (May–October), the average temperature is 28 °C, and in winter the temperature rarely drops below 20 °C. Rain is more frequent between June and October, when hurricanes can also occur.The main tourist season is November to April.

Currency. The Bahamian dollar is pegged to the US dollar. It is divided into 100 cents, and the most frequently used coins are 1, 5, 10 and 25 cents; banknotes 1, 5, 10, 20, 50 and $100. U.S dollars and major credit cards are widely accepted in the larger establishments. Euros can be exchanged in banks and casinos.

Customs allowance. Visitors aged 18 and over can import duty-free 200 cigarettes or 50 cigars or 1 lb tobacco, 1 US quart of spirits and 1 US quart of wine, as well as other articles for a maximum value of US$100.

Electricity. The voltage is 120 V, 60 Hz, as in North America; plugs have two flat prongs.

Emergencies. For fire, police or ambulance services, call 911 or 919.

Internet. There are booths offering internet access at Prince George Wharf, and free wi-fi is available from numerous bars and restaurants in Nassau and Freeport.

Language. The official language is English.

Telephone. Nassau (area code 242) is linked to the US network. To call the UK, dial 011 44, then the area code (minus the first zero) and the local number. Note that roaming costs for using your mobile phone can be high and dedicated long distance phones can be expensive too; it may be better to use a pay phone or purchase a local SIM card.

Time. Standard time is UTC/GMT−5 with Daylight Saving Time (UTC/GMT−4) from the 2nd Sunday in March to the 1st Sunday in November.

Transport. A quick and easy way of getting around Nassau and Freeport is to take a cheap minibus known as a jitney. With its long, straight roads, Grand Bahama is a great place to explore on a scooter. There are rental kiosks along the main roads in Freeport/Lucaya, and helmets are included. Taxis are also freely available, though renting a car can work out cheaper. Traffic drives on the left.

The intense colours of paradise: quaint bungalows overlook a turquoise sea.

hemis.fr/Frances

TURKS AND CAICOS

This idyllic string of dots at the end of the Bahamas chain is sometimes called the last frontier. Ruins of old plantations, mysterious caves and shabby but beautifully quaint wooden bungalows are as easy to find as the gold- and white-sand beaches stretching around the islands.

Turks Islands

The Turks form a chain of 12 small islands which stretches like a necklace of pearls for barely 40 km (25 miles) from north to south. The islands' white sandy beaches recall the natural salt which was once collected here. Cockburn Town, the capital and main centre of Turks and Caicos, is situated on the largest island of Grand Turk.

Grand Turk

The somewhat rocky eastern coast is countered by undulating dunes on the island's western shore. It is said to be one of the world's best spots for scuba-diving, and there's excellent sport fishing for everything from sailfish and marlin to wahoo and kingfish. Places such as Gibbs' Cay and the Grand Turk Natural Marine Park have intricate reefs and plenty of colourful fish and sponges.

Cockburn Town

Known to out-islanders as "the city", the capital provides a striking combination of elegance and hustle and bustle: its venerable 200-year-old limestone **Church of St Thomas** sits happily in the lap of the islands' business centre.

The best way to see the town is by donkey carriage. The handsome buggies, elaborately carved, will take you in style through the historic areas of **Duke Street**, the main thoroughfare, and **Front Street**, where three-storey houses of wood and limestone in typical West Indian style line the seafront. Stop off at the old **Victoria Public Library** to see its fascinating collection of reference books relating to local history.

On Front Street, the **Turks and Caicos National Museum** occupies a 18th-century residence, Guinea House. Its key exhibit is the Molasses Reef Wreck, an early 16th-century Spanish caravel.

TURKS AND CAICOS FLASHBACK

16th–17th centuries
In 1512 Spanish explorer Ponce de León discovers Grand Turk, inhabited by Lucayan Indians. The islands are used as pirates' hideaways. Using slave labour, Bermudian traders, the first whites to settle permanently here, begin collecting natural sea salt for sale to the British colonies in America.

18th–19th centuries
Despite a 1710 Spanish invasion and three French invasions, the Bermudians keep returning to the islands and rebuilding their salt pans. In 1766, the Turks and Caicos are placed under the control of the Bahamas, a British colony. During the American Revolution, British loyalists flee to the Caicos, where they plant sisal and cotton. The islands separate from the Bahamas in 1848, but in 1874 they become a dependency of Jamaica.

20th century–present
John Glenn, the first American to orbit the planet, splashes down off the coast of Grand Turk in 1962. That year the islands win independence from Jamaica but are linked for administrative purposes with the Bahamas. In 1972 they receive their own governor as a British Crown Colony. Hotels spring up, including luxury resorts. The economy, dependent on fishing, tourism and offshore banking, suffers severe setbacks in 2008 as a result of the global financial crisis. The next year, following accusations of corruption at the heart of the administrative centre, the UK suspends power, formerly largely autonomous, and introduces a governor. The elections of November 2012 end the guardianship and mark the return of a local government heading the archipelago.

flickr.com/West

museum also documents the salt industry and displays artefacts of the Lucayan Indians. Elsewhere in town, **Her Majesty's Prison** was built in the 19th century to house escaped slaves and was still operating as a jail until the 1990s. Today you can tour its austere cells.

Around Cockburn Town

South of town, the **Grand Turk Cruise Centre** at the cruise ship dock offers pools with private cabanas plus bars, restaurants and shopping. There are lovely white sands at **Governor's Beach** and the even prettier **Pillory Beach**.

Right up in the northern tip of the island, Grand Turk's cast-iron **lighthouse** is its best-known landmark. Built in 1852 on the order of the US government to prevent the shipwrecks that had plagued the island's northern coastline, its lamps were originally designed to run on whale oil, but were converted to run on electricity in 1971. It's no longer in operation but you can stroll in the grounds. Just offshore is the spot where, in 1962, US astronaut **John Glenn**'s capsule touched down after orbiting the earth; there's a replica at the cruise-ship pier.

The Cays

Pennington Cay, **Gibbs Cay** and **Round ›4Cay** have sanctuaries where you'll see some interesting bird and butterfly species.

Hummingbirds need to feed all day long to survive. | Mangoes, ripe for the picking.

Salt Cay

Salt Cay, 14 km (9 miles) from Grand Turk, is the most charming of all the salt islands. Accessible by boat and only five minutes away by air, it has fine beaches and old windmills next to the long-abandoned salt ponds. On the island's west side there are two small villages, complete with a school and several churches to serve the island's population of 80. Descendants of salt rakers own the **White House**, is furnished with the original antique pieces.

DINING AND SHOPPING

On the menu

The star of Turks and Caicos cuisine is the conch, which appears in fritters, chowder, cracked, dried, creoled and curried. It is closely rivalled by the lobster, deliciously barbecued.

Native dishes are more modest but no less appealing: hominy (grits) cooked with peas or dried conch, accompanied by fish, chicken and vegetables, or peas and rice flavoured with salt beef and pig's tail. A favourite at weekends is johnnycake (a sort of pancake made with cornmeal) served with boiled fish. Chicken, pork, fish and goat are often cooked in jerk sauce, a rich and tasty blend of onions, herbs, spices, hot pepper and garlic.

Rum punch is one of the most popular drinks; a heady concoction of Lucayan rum, coconut, orange and pineapple juice and grenadine syrup.

The best buys

The best island for shopping is Provo. Local crafts include woven baskets of straw or sea grass, polished conch shells (made into flower vases, candle-holders and fruit bowls),

naive Haitian-style paintings, woodcarvings, dolls and metal-work—including unusual objects made from recycled oil drums. You'll also find chic resortwear, hats and bags, and a wide selection of dive and snorkel accessories.

Among gourmet ideas, look for Caribbean rums and the unique Caribbean Lobster Oil, made from sunflower oil infused with aromatic herbs, tomatoes and the flavour of local lobster. It can be used in a salad dressing, as a marinade, for cooking fish and seafood or for adding flavour to pasta and rice.

Duty-free perfumes, watches, jewellery, crystal and gift items are sold in six outlets, as well as the airport. At the Philatelic Bureaus on Grand Turk and Provo you will find lovely collectors' postage stamps, T-shirts, post-cards and other souvenirs.

Caicos Islands

The Caicos Islands lie at the very end of the Bahamas chain, remote and essentially undiscovered. Some 40,000 residents live on eight of these 30 islands; most of them are settled on Providenciales Island. English is the official language, although some of the locals still speak Creole. The inhabitants, mainly descendants of African slaves, are called "Belongers". They indeed belong to the island, just as the island belongs to them. Yet this name also refers to a specific status, only acquired by the people who have close ties to the island.

South Caicos

Humpback whales put on a spectacular sight from January to March when they wend their way, during their southern migration, through the **Turks Island Passage** which separates the islands of Turks and the more westerly Caicos. By boat or a 10-minute flight, you can hop over this passage from Grand Turk to South Caicos, the most populated island in the days of the salt trade. Lively **Cockburn Harbour**, the only town, is the main fishing port. There are several fishing plants on this island, where lobster, conch and fish are processed for local consumption and for export.

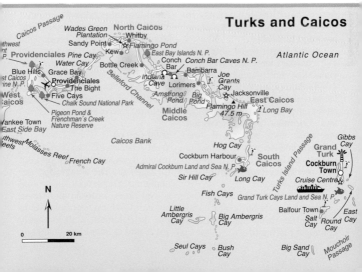

East Caicos

Once home to a sisal plantation, East Caicos is inhabited only by a small community of Haitians and is largely given over the the mangrove and swamp. On the north coast there is a superb beach, where turtles lay their eggs (luckily they are left in peace by humans who are wary of the large mosquito population).

Jacksonville, the only town, lies in ruins in the northwest of the island. In nearby caves, petroglyphs show that the island was inhabited centuries ago.

Middle Caicos

Middle Caicos (or Grand Caicos) is the largest of the islands, but only sparsely populated with fewer than 300 inhabitants in three settlements: **Conch Bar**, **Bambarra** and **Lorimers**.

On the north coast there are extraordinary **limestone caves** with stalactites and stalagmites. In 1978, American archaeologists came to the islands to explore the caves and ruins near Bambarra and Lorimers and discovered artefacts and relics of the Lucayan and Arawak Indians, the islands' earliest settlers. One site near **Armstrong Pond** contains a Lucayan ball court.

The island's southern coast supports a frigate bird colony and a large blue hole that supports abundant marine life.

North Caicos

North Caicos, the "Garden Island" is known for its growing tourist development along a 9-km (6-mile) beach and for its bone-fishing waters. Its villages are **Bottle Creek** to the east, **Whitby** in the north, **Sandy Point** in the northwest and **Kew** in the centre, close to the haunting **Wades Green Plantation**.

Pine Cay

Privately owned Pine Cay has an exquisite beach stretching for 4 km (2.5 miles) opposite the **Caicos Cays National Underwater Park**. Hiking on the island's trails, you'll encounter colonial ruins. Nearby **Water Cay** and **Little Water Cay** are rich with shells.

Providenciales Island

Most of the major tourist infra-structure—as well as processing plants for spiny lobster and conch—is centred on Providenciales Island, referred to by the locals as "Provo". The most beautiful of its beaches are in the north near **Grace Bay**.

West Caicos

West Caicos, 22 sq km (9 sq miles) in area, is uninhabited but for seabirds. The abandoned settlement of **Yankee Town** lies around a sisal press, railroad and steam engine. Dive operators come to this quiet haven, with its sandy coves and crystal-clear waters.

THE HARD FACTS

Climate. The Turks and Caicos are accustomed to a very dry climate, with more humidity occuring in North Caicos. The averagetemperature is 27–29°C November to May, 29–32°C between June and October, with peaks of 35°C in the height of summer, though the trade winds allow alr to circulate. The stormy season runs from June to November.

Clothing. Take light clothing made of cotton or linen and a waterproof coat or umbrella for the rainy season. A lightweight but warm sweater is useful for the cooler evenings.

Currency. The official currency is the US dollar. Major credit cards are accepted by most hotels, restaurants and taxi services.

Electricity. Electric devices operate at 110/60 volts, 60 Hz. Plugs have 2 flat prongs. An adaptor and transformer are necessary for European devices.

Emergencies. For police, fire and ambulance, call 911.

Language. The official language is English; a little Creole is equally spoken.

Time difference. The islands follow UTC/GMT–5, with daylight saving time (UTC/GMT–4) from April to October.

Tipping. Top waiters, taxi drivers and porters 15 percent.

Transport. Two airlines operate flights daily between Providenciales and Grand Turk (taking 30 min), as well as to Salt Cay and South Caicos (less frequently). There is no regular ferry service. Tour operators offer packages to visit islands and cays. Taxis are available at the port and the airport, jeeps and scooters are available to rent on Grand Turk and Providenciales. Driving is on the left. Only parts of the roads are tarmaced.

Water. Drink only bottled mineral water and it is advisable to also use it for cleaning your teeth. Water used for making ice should be boiled or sterilized.

istockphoto.com/Pershern

Turquoise sea and golden sands, all the
promise of a tropical island.

istockphoto.com/Moore

GREATER ANTILLES

The Greater Antilles islands laze in the sun! Cuba, Jamaica, Hispaniola (divided between the Dominican Republic and Haiti), Puerto Rico and Cayman Islands—still bear the mark of conquistadors. The sleepy Caymans sprinkle the sea about 300 km (180 miles) northwest of Jamaica. Grand Cayman is the largest of the three, followed by Cayman Brac and Little Cayman.

Cayman Islands

Most of the points of interest in the islands are on Grand Cayman, an important centre for offshore finance, with hundreds of banks and insurance companies located in the capital, George Town. The other islands are a loner's paradise. The swimming is great, so is the snorkelling, and the diving has a strong claim to being the best in the Caribbean. One of the most popular scuba sites is Spanish Bay Reef, replete with intricate corals and brightly coloured fish.

Beyond the reefs are the big fish such as bluefin tuna, marlin and wahoo. Bonito, amberjack and barracuda are closer to shore and inside the reef you'll land grouper and yellow-tailed snapper. Boats can be rented, ranging from an 18-m yacht to a dinghy.

Grand Cayman

The largest town in the archipelago, home to some 28,000 inhabitants, quiet **George Town** holds the **Cayman Islands National Museum**, which gives a good overview of the island's history and culture. On Esterley Tibbetts Highway, a handsome new building houses the excellent **National Gallery**, with works from local artists and innovative temporary exhibitions. North of George Town's well-planned streets, **Seven Mile Beach** (a bit shorter, actually) is overlooked by hotels and boasts clean white sand and clear blue sea.

Just inland, the 23 m **Camana Bay Observation Tower** offers stunning views over the pancake-flat island. You could take the lift to the top, but the staircase is an experience in itself, with a wall mosaic representing a dive from seabed to surface.

CAYMAN FLASHBACK

16th century
Columbus discovers the Caymans in 1503, calling the group "Las Tortugas" after the great number of turtles in the surrounding seas. Early Spanish settlers of the Caribbean area rename them the "Caimán" islands, possibly mistaking the native iguanas for alligators.

17th–18th centuries
In 1670 the Caymans are formally ceded to Great Britain by Spain. About the same time, the islands' first permanent settlers arrive, an assortment of debtors, buccaneers hiding from the Royal Navy, deserters from Cromwell's army and sailors shipwrecked on the islands' reefs. They make their living by working small plantations (later with the help of slaves) or by fishing.

19th century–present
By an Act of Parliament in 1863, the Governor and legislature of Jamaica are given certain legislative powers in the Islands. When Jamaica chooses independence in 1962, the Caymans elect to become a British Crown Colony. Today, they are an important international financial centre, with a thriving economy and one of the highest per capita incomes in the Caribbean. Their official status is now that of UK Dependent Territory.

hemis.fr/Renault

Grand Cayman

Little Cayman, Cayman Brac

Austin Conolly Rd

Colliers

Colliers Pond

Sand Bluff

Gun Bay

Blake's Ridgefield

East End

Blue Iguana Nature Reserve

Salina Reserve

Great Beach

Lighthouse

East End Marshland Natural Habitat

Queen Elizabeth II Botanic Park

Half Moon Bay

High Rock

Blow Holes

Old Robin Point

Old Robin Rd

Old Man Bay

Sea View Rd

Cottage Point

White Sand Bay

Frank Sound

Frank Sound Rd

Frank Sound Point

North Side

Malportas Pond

Caribbean Sea

Grape Tree Point

Driftwood

Brinkleys Drive

Central Mangrove Wetland

Betty Bay Point

Breakers

Midland Acres Town

Pease Bay

Belford Estates

Bodden Town

Rum Point

Rum Point Channel

Cayman Kai

Water Cay

Little Sound

Booby Cay

Duck Pond Cay

North Sound Estates

Northward

Pedro

Newlands

Savannah

Shamrock Rd

Old Jones Rd

Pedro St James National Historical Ste

Spotts

Rum Point Main Channel

Stingray City

North Sound

North Sound Ferry

Spanish Reef Bay

Big Channel

Conch Point

Palmetto Point

Barkers

Head of Barkers

Barkers National Park

Governors Harbour

West Bay

Yacht Club

Water Ground

Hell

North West Point

Cayman Turtle Farm

Esterly Tibbetts Hwy

West Bay Rd

Seven Mile Beach

Camana Bay

Observation Tower

National Gallery

1919 Peace Memorial

George Town

Cruise Port

Cayman Islands National Museum

Barcadere

George Town Golf Course

Owen Roberts International Airport

Tropical Gardens Rd

Red Bay Estates

South Sound Rd

Prospect

South Sound

South West Point

Pull-and-Be-Damned Point

Sand Cay

N

0   5 km

DINING AND SHOPPING

On the menu

Try turtle in tasty soups or stews, or the truly memorable steaks. Conch, a dense and nourishing sea-snail, turns up in hearty stews and chowders and also as a marinated cocktail. Spiny lobster often appears as an appetizer, garnished with seaweed. Codfish and ackee is another local favourite, sometimes eaten for breakfast. The rosy ackee fruit is poisonous until it ripens and bursts open, revealing a delicate yellow interior. When cooked, it tastes somewhat like scrambled eggs. Your vegetable might be white sweet potato, breadfruit, cassava root or fried plantain, a larger, coarser cousin of the banana. Rice is frequently cooked up with coconut milk and with red beans (rice'n'peas).

For dessert, sample some of the exotic local fruits: mango, papaya (paw paw), coconut, sweetsop and soursop. The light, aromatic rum of the Caribbean is rightly famous, and forms the base of many cocktails and punches. The popular piña colada consists of rum, coconut cream, crushed pineapple (or juice) and crushed ice. Rum punch is a refreshing concoction of lime juice, sugar syrup and crushed ice, with a sprinkling of nutmeg or bitters.

The best buys

There are two shopping categories on the islands—local handicrafts and imported duty-free articles. Look for the jewellery fashioned from shells and local semi-precious stones like caymanite, found only in these islands and veined with shades of orange, brown, cream and black. Other local items include numismatic jewellery crafted from old coins retrieved from sunken vessels and featured in exquisite gold and diamond settings. Straw work is another popular craft, and you'll find a broad range of woven goods such as hats, coasters and hammocks.

flickr.com/angelcandy.baby

To the North

Continue along the coast road to the **Cayman Turtle Farm**, a marine theme park incorporating the island's original turtle breeding and research facility, where touch tanks allow you to handle green turtles. Here you can also find souvenir shops and restaurants.

Other entertaining attractions include a saltwater predator lagoon with underwater viewing panels, a huge pool and the **Cayman Street** living museum.

Afterwards you may as well go to...**Hell**, a Dantesque area of jagged black limestone formations; you can by postcards and have them postmarked here to prove you have seen what life is like in Hell.

On the northwest tip, pristine **Barkers National Park** beach is a beautiful and secluded spot. To the east, in the protected waters of North Sound, is **Stingray City**, a series of shallow sandbars. Southern stingrays congregate in the crystalline waters, nuzzling and brushing against the divers feeding them. Visitors canbsnorkel with the fish, take an excursion boat or watch from an observatory.

istockphoto.com/Jacobson

istockphoto.com/Semet

istockphoto.com/Argalis

Directions leading to Hell in Grand Cayman. | A blue spotted stingray cruises the seabed as it feeds. | Lake at the Queen Elizabeth II Botanic Park, Grand Cayman.

A blow hole near East End, Grand-Cayman, sprays a fountain of sea.

To the East

Pedro St James National Historic Site was built by an Englishman who arrived here in 1765. Local stories also associate it with the pirate Henry Morgan and a 17th-century Spaniard, Pedro Gómez. It has now been restored as a living museum with a 3D multi-sensory theatre which retells the history of the house and of the Caymans; there are also lush gardens and lovely views.

At the **Blow Holes** near East End, sprays of water shoot like geysers through sea-torn rocks. Further on, the wrecks begin: more than 325 have been counted around the island. The most southerly, off the east coast, is the *Ridgefield,* visible from the road.

Cutting through the centre of the island to Grand Cayman's north side, **Frank Sound Road** passes the turnoff for **Queen Elizabeth II Botanic Park**, home to beautiful gardens and the **Blue Iguana Habitat**, where you will see many of the turquoise lizards for which the Caymans are famed.

At the north coast, turn left to reach **Rum Point** and **Cayman Kai**, where the whole landscape shines blue and silver. The silky sand has been divided up and very pleasant beach houses have been built, many surrounded by beautiful flower-filled gardens.

Cayman Brac

Uninhabited until 1833, the island now has a population of some 1700 Cayman Brackers. The name is Gaelic for bluff, a cliff that rises sheer from the water to about 43 m. At **Stake Bay**, the **Cayman Brac Museum** displays sundry cooking utensils, ship-building tools and other items contributed by the islanders themselves. There are several resorts, with services for scuba diving and snorkelling.

Little Cayman

About 200 people live here on 26 sq km (10 sq miles) of silence and fragrant breezes—providing a haven for birds and blue iguanas. Accommodation consists of a few small club-style hotels and private cottages. Civilization is slowly encroaching, yet great excitement still greets a landing of the plane from Grand Cayman, bringing guests, mail and gossip from the outside world.

THE HARD FACTS

Climate. The Caymans bask in a warm, tropical climate, with temperatures moderated by trade winds. The rainy season is May to October.

Clothing. Pack lightweight cottons and linens and a raincoat or umbrella for the the rainy season. Warmer clothes are useful for evenings.

Communications. The islands are linked to the US network. Country code for Cayman Islands 1 345, for Turks and Caicos 1 649. The international access code from the Cayman Islands is 00. There are public phone booths throughout the islands which take widely available prepaid cards. Phoning home via one of these will be cheaper than using your mobile phone, as roaming is expensive. Internet access is available at most large hotels, many of which have free wi-fi, as do many cafés, bars and restaurants.

Currency. The Cayman Islands dollar (CI$ or KYD) is divided into 100 cents. Coins range from 1 to 25 cents, banknotes from 1 to 100 dollars. Shops will also accept British Pounds and US and Canadian dollars.

Driving. Traffic drives on the left. A good road network connects the coastal towns of all three main Cayman Islands, where drivers must be over 25 and speed limits are strictly enforced.

Electricity. 110 volts AC, 50 Hz. Plugs have two flat pins.

Emergencies. Call 911 for the police service and fire brigade.

Language. English is the official language, with minority local dialects also spoken.

Time. UTC/GMT−5, all year round.

Transport. Airports: Owen Roberts International Airport, Grand Cayman (GCM; 2 km east of Georgetown); Gerard Smith Airport, Cayman Brac (CYB; 8 km from West End); Grand Turk Airport, Grand Turk (GDT; 3 km south of Cockburn Town). A flight from Gran Cayman to Cayman Brac takes 30 mnutes. For information on buses, taxis and car rental, visit: www.caymanislands.co.uk/planatrip/transportation.aspx.

Water. It is advisable to stick to bottled mineral water, which is widely available.

Today's Jamaicans underline the truth of
the motto "out of many, one people".

Jamaica

Jamaica lies some 150 km (90 miles) south of Cuba and is the third-largest Caribbean island after Cuba and Hispaniola (shared between Haiti and the Dominican Republic): 235 km (145 miles) long and 82 km (51 miles) at its widest part. The capital and commercial centre is Kingston, situated on the south coast and backed by the Blue and John Crow Mountains, designated a UNESCO World Heritage site in 2015 for their biodiversity and rich cultural heritage . An array of stunning resorts with picturesque sand beaches extends along the north coast. The original inhabitants, peaceful Arawak Indians, called it Xamayaca, Land of Wood and Water.

Kingston

Jamaica's exuberant capital is everything you would expect a busy Caribbean port city to be— crowded and lively, with an occasionally aggressive energy.

Kingston throbs to the sound of bass-heavy reggae and the calls of the island's 200 species of birds. Dreadlocked Rastafarians mingle with besuited office workers, while jelly coconuts and soft drinks are sold from painted handcarts. Exotic smells fill the air, from tropical flowers to spicy fried fish. And ever present in the distance is the outline of the Blue Mountains, wreathed with trailing mists.

Founded by survivors of the Port Royal earthquake of 1692, Kingston soon expanded and became the seat of Jamaica's as its principal port. It still has some fine colonial-style buildings. The city falls into two sections— Downtown Kingston and New Kingston, where the ground rises towards the cooler, airy foothills of the Blue Mountains.

New Kingston

This uptown district of hotels, banks, offices and shops also holds some of the city's loveliest houses, with lace-like verandas and wooden decoration. On Hope Road, **Devon House** was built in 1881 by George Stiebel, one of the first black millionaires in the Caribbean. The government has refurbished it after the style of different historical periods. The former staff quarters now house craft shops and restaurants— don't leave without trying the famous Jamaican patties and locally made ice-cream.

The **Bob Marley Museum**, 56 Hope Road, has been set up in the reggae musician's former home and studio, and documents his life and works (he died in Miami in 1981). The Tuff Gong record label was founded here by The Wailers in 1970.

East along Hope and Old Hope roads, the **Hope Botanical Gardens** are the largest in the Caribbean.

JAMAICA FLASHBACK

15th–16th centuries
Columbus sights the north coast of Jamaica in 1494 and lands in Montego Bay. During his fourth voyage (1502–04) he is marooned for a year at St Ann's Bay. In 1510 the Spanish found a settlement nearby, Sevilla la Nueva. Fever drives the settlers to the south coast, the site of today's Spanish Town. During the 150 years of Spanish colonial rule, the original 60,000-strong Arawak population is wiped out by disease and massacre. African slaves are brought in to replace them as a labour force.

17th century
The British land in Kingston Harbour (1655) and capture Jamaica. The Spanish governor heads for the hills, where he carries on a guerrilla resistance for five years. The Treaty of Madrid (1670) sets an official seal on England's claim to Jamaica. Escaping slaves who take refuge in the hills—the Maroons—harass the British.

18th century
Sugar brings prosperity to British planters, but slave uprisings in response to brutal plantation conditions are common. In 1739 the British sign a treaty with the Maroons, granting them certain privileges and independence, and thus putting a stop to the intermittent warfare. By 1785, Jamaica has a population of 25,000 whites and 250,000 slaves.

19th century
Jamaica's last and most serious slave rebellion occurs in Montego Bay in 1831. Slavery is abolished by Parliament in 1833 but the system does not actually die out for another 50 years. As the sugar industry begins its decline, the living conditions of the emancipated slaves grow ever worse, and a minor revolt in 1865 to obtain justice meets with swift reprisals. Jamaica is named a Crown Colony in 1866.

20th century–present
Thanks to the newly developed banana trade, the discovery of bauxite and growing tourism, the economy experiences a lift. Jamaica is granted its own constitution and self-government in 1944. On August 6, 1962, the island becomes independent but remains part of the British Commonwealth and a lively democracy.

Downtown Kingston

The waterfront's skyscrapers are mostly the preserve of office workers. Jamaica's excellent **National Gallery**, located on Ocean Boulevard, comprises contemporary paintings and sculpture alongside Spanish and English colonial art.

Craft Market

Near the National Gallery is Kingston's Craft Market, set in a cavernous warehouse building. This is the spot to look for bargains in basketry, carving, jewellery and colourful clothing featuring Jamaica's distinctive flag.

Parish Church

Kingston Parish Church on South Parade dates back to 1699, but was devastated by the 1907 earthquake. It has now been completely rebuilt, but still contains the black marble gravestone of Admiral Benbow, who died in 1702 after battle with the French.

Port Royal

The route out to Port Royal passes along the Kingston waterfront, past the hot-spring pools at **Rockfort Mineral Baths** and along the Palisadoes, a ribbon-thin landspit enclosing the Kingston Harbour.

In the late 17th century, Boston and Port Royal were the largest cities of the English colonies in the New World. Port Royal, built

Travel Pictures Ltd

hemis.fr/Degas

Two sights for sore eyes along Hope Road: Devon House and the Bob Marley Museum.

on a sandy peninsula, was known as "the wickedest city on earth". Here the pirates caroused, rum and money flowed freely, pleasure was sweet, and death often quick and violent. And then, suddenly, on June 7, 1692, a devastating earthquake hit: buildings toppled and two-thirds of the town sank beneath the sea. The disaster claimed the lives of over a thousand people, and legend has it that on stormy days you can still hear the tolling of submerged church bells.

Excavations of the underwater city began in the 1980s, mainly focusing on buildings on Lime Street, inland from the harbour. The site is one of the richest 17th-century archaeological sites in the world and is currently on the UNESCO's World Heritage tentative list.

St Peter's Church

Built in 1725, it replaced the earlier churches which disappeared in the earthquake and ensuing fire. Outside is the tomb of Louis Galdy, a French refugee from religious persecution. During the 1692 earthquake he was swallowed into a yawning crack in the ground and thrown out again into the sea, where he swam to a boat and managed to save himself.

Fort Charles

Once commanded by Nelson, this is the only one of the six original forts to have survived Port Royal's manifold disasters. It was founded in 1656 and named after Charles II of England. The prow-shaped fort once stood at the water's edge, but land movements have shifted it to an inland position. Two small museums display artefacts uncovered

View over Fort Charles, Port Royal. | Coffee from the Blue Mountains is some of the best in the world.

from the sunken city. Behind the main building, the fort's ammunition store has been listing at an angle since 1907, when part of it sank into the ground. It is now known as **Giddy House**.

Other Buildings

Close to the fort, on Old Gaol Street, the sturdy cut-stone **Old Gaol House** is a former women's prison, still standing as firm as in its 17th century heyday. Beyond here, on New Street, the ramshackle **Old Naval Hospital** is the oldest prefabricated structure in the New World, its iron structure having been shipped over from the UK and erected here in 1819.

Lime Cay

From Port Royal's Morgan's Harbour Hotel, you can jump in a water taxi to Lime Cay, a gorgeous little scrap of sandy beach surrounded by crystal waters that offer some lovely snorkelling. A popular getaway for locals, it is most lively at the weekends.

Spanish Town

Jamaica's old capital is set on the banks of the River Cobre. The Spanish called it Villa de La Vega, "town on the plain". The only thing Spanish about it now is the name, but the **Cathedral Church of St Jago de la Vega** stands on the site of a Spanish chapel demolished by Oliver Cromwell's sol-

diers. Head next to the graceful Parade Square, designed by the British as the town's centrepiece. A plaque on the wall of the former governor's residence, **King's House**, commemorates the end of the slave trade in 1838.

On the north side of the square is a John Bacon memorial to Admiral George Rodney, who saved Jamaica from French invasion in 1782. On the south side stands the 19th-century courthouse. On the eastern side, the colonnaded red-brick and wood structure is the **House of Assembly**, erected in the 1760s.

Blue Mountains

These cool, misty mountains are easily accessible from Kingston. Head through Papine to The Cooperage, where the road forks; turn right for **Mavis Bank**, from where you can make the tough but superlative four-hour trek up to the 2,256 m **Blue Mountain Peak**. You climb through lush and twisted foliage wreathed in pale mountain mists which clear to reveal stunning vistas. The hike starts at 1 a.m. so that you reach the peak in time for sunset; wear sturdy shoes and warm clothes, and always go with a guide.

Turning left at The Cooperage leads to the military training camp at **Newcastle** and to the hiking trails and city views of beautiful **Holywell National Park**.

DINING AND SHOPPING

On the menu

Two soups to try are pepperpot, containing callaloo (spinach-like greens), okra and coconut milk, and the rich, creamy pumpkin soup. "Stamp and go" are fried fishcakes. Solomon Gundy is a well-seasoned pickled herring. You'll find patties—meat or veg-filled pastries—everywhere.

The ingredients of Jamaica's national dish, saltfish and ackee, are not indigenous. The fish was originally imported from Norway as cheap protein for slaves, and the creamy yellow ackee fruit was brought to the island by Captain Bligh.

Jerk pork and chicken—highly peppered meat that has been smoked over pimento wood—is a speciality of the east coast. The recipe came from the runaway Maroons, who originally used it on wild boar.

Cho-cho is a prickly fruit with a taste like marrow. Green bananas can be boiled, while their sweet cousins the plantains are sliced and fried.

Coconut water makes a good roadside refresher. The green fruit is beheaded with a clean sweep of the machete and you drink straight from the nut.

Red Stripe beer is the local lager, but Jamaica's most famous drink is rum. Light and aromatic, it's very popular in a planter's punch combined with lime juice, sugar syrup and crushed ice.

The best buys

Local products worth considering include fashions, embroidery, shell work, handcrafted jewellery, woodcarvings, jams and spices. If you suddenly feel the urge to grow dreadlocks, save time by buying a beret with a fringe of Rastafarian locks attached. You'll spot some fine Rastafarian carvings. Look for objects made of lignum vitae, a light-coloured hardwood. And take home a CD of reggae music and a bottle of golden rum or Tia Maria (a coffee and chocolate liqueur). Or why not some Blue Mountain coffee, said to be the best in the world?

fotolia.com/Clochard

Resorts

Each of these resorts, dotted along the north coast of the island, has in its way contributed to Jamaica's well-deserved reputation as a prime holiday destination. The earliest testimonial to Jamaica was given in 1494, when Christopher Columbus landed on the island: he described it as "the fairest island that eyes have beheld".

Port Antonio and around

Regularly refreshed by rain showers, Port Antonio, on the northeast coast, about 100 km (60 miles) from Kingston, is one of the greenest spots in Jamaica. It was an early mecca for tourism, well before anyone had heard of Montego Bay or Ocho Rios, and offers a feeling of exclusivity and secluded charm.

Cradled by the arms of the Blue Mountains, Port Antonio has two superb harbours, divided by the Titchfield Peninsula. On its tip rises **Fort George**, built to protect the original settlement; today its walls enclose a school.

Offshore, palm-wreathed **Navy Island** was once owned by the film star Errol Flynn (1909–59), after whom the town's marina, with its restaurants and waterside promenades, has been named.

The thriving waters off Port Antonio are noted for deep-sea fishing.

Bonnie View

A walk up to Bonnie View is rewarded with a splendid panorama of the town and twin bays, the multicoloured reefs shimmering under turquoise seas.

Folly Point

Head east of town to the huge ruined shell of the Folly (1905), a once grand mansion built by American billionaire Alfred Mitchell. In 1938 the roof caved in after the house fell prey to sea salt, which corroded its iron reinforcing rods.

Rafting on the Rio Grande. No visit to Jamaica is complete without a raft trip down the Rio Grande, between the slopes of the Blue Mountains. Originally, the bamboo rafts were used by banana plantation owners to transport their produce to the port. On holidays the planters liked to coast along with family and friends. It was Errol Flynn who first hit on the idea of having a raft fitted with seats to make the ride more comfortable. A qualified rafter navigates the rapids, giving you the chance to marvel at the luxuriant jungle scenery. A three-hour trip departs from Berridale and glides beneath the foliage to Rafter's Rest at the mouth of the river, marking the end of the 11-km (7-mile) trip.

East of Port Antonio

Don't miss a visit to **Blue Lagoon**, also known as Blue Hole, southeast of Port Antonio. Translucent water of the deepest ultramarine lies surrounded by dark vegetation.

Past the lovely beaches at **Frenchman's Cove**, **Winnifred Bay** and **Long Bay**, **Reach Falls** is a fantastic spot for a swim, with cool waters cascading into a deep, wide pool. Changing facilities and refreshments are available.

Ocho Rios Region

The region embraces a golden strip about 100 km (60 miles) long between Annotto and Discovery bays and is considered one of the most important tourist havens in Jamaica.

Port Maria and Oracabessa

The road west from Annotto Bay leads to Port Maria, an old banana port, where there are some lovely views over the shoreline.

Both Port Maria and Oracabessa, another banana port, gained fame through two celebrated British writers who settled in the region. Ian Fleming (1908–1964) married in Port Maria's town hall and wrote his James Bond novels at his estate, *Goldeneye* in Oracabessa, now a luxury hotel. A strip of shoreline here, James Bond Beach, is open to the public. Fleming's *Dr No* (1958) was filmed in Jamaica, part of it in the old bauxite factory at Ocho Rios.

The home of Sir Noël Coward (1899–1973), **Firefly**, stands on a headland near Port Maria. He died here in 1973 and is buried at the bottom of the garden under a marble slab. The house has been left much as it was in Coward's lifetime, with his belongings still in the cabinets and his paintings on the walls. The gardens afford stunning views of the coastline, Port Maria Bay and of the rolling inland hills.

Prospect Outback Adventures

This slick visitor attraction offers horse and camel rides, segway tours and jitney rides through the working fruit plantation. You can also take Jamaican cooking classes at the Great House, feed a flock of ostriches and take and adventurous "mud-buggy" safari.

Ocho Rios Town

Ocho Rios offers a vast choice of activities: scuba diving, deep-sea fishing, golf, shopping sprees at **Island Village** and the **Craft Market**, exploring the central **Turtle River Park**, or just some swimming and sunbathing. At the **Konoko Falls**, paths wander past pools filled with koi carp and turtles, and a museum covers local history; you can also climb a waterfall and explore the aviary. Nearby, **Shaw Park Botanical Gardens**, besides lawns and terraces of tropical flora, birds and waterfalls, offer a splendid view of Ocho Rios Bay and the surrounding countryside.

Mystic Mountain
Just outside town, you can take a chairlift through the forest canopy up to an entertainment complex with a pool, restaurants, a treetop zipwire and an aerial bobsleigh run, inspired by Jamaica's Olympic team.

Dunn's River Falls
Along the coast to the west, this is the loveliest, most refreshing spot around. Clear, cool water from the rainforest comes cascading down over limestone terraces through pools to the sea. You can climb the falls assisted by experienced guides, or take the steps with handrails and wooden observation decks. Opposite the falls you can swim with dolphins and explore nature trails at **Dolphin Cove**.

St Ann's Bay
This is the capital of the parish of the same name. You can watch polo at **Drax Hall** east of town; matches are held every Saturday. Nearby **Chukka Caribbean Adventures** offer all sorts of adventurous activities, from horse-riding in the sea to zip-lining and river-tubing. To the west, **Seville** was the site of Jamaica's first Spanish settlement, Sevilla Nueva, founded in 1509,

hemis.fr

You can climb from the beach all the way to the top of Dunn's River Falls.

and is on UNESCO's tentative list. The Seville Great House has a museum displaying Taino Indian artefacts found here and recreations of early settlements.

Fans of reggae music head inland, via Claremont, Bonneville and Alderton, to **Nine Miles**, site of the **Bob Marley Mausoleum**, where the king of reggae is buried with his guitar. Adorned with stained-glass windows, his marble mausoleum makes a sharp contrast to the adjacent humble hut, with its single bed, where the international cult figure was born.

Runaway Bay

A line-up of hotels fringes the shores of Runaway Bay. The limestone **Runaway Caves and Green Grotto**, first used by the Arawak Indians, later became a pirate and smugglers' haunt and then a place of refuge for runaway slaves; more recently it held a nightclub, now closed to protect the cave structure and its resident bats.

A visit to the caves takes you 36 m underground, past stalagmites, stalactites and a tiny lake. It is fed by channels connected to the sea, and the water level rises and falls with the tides.

This part of the coast is replete with memories of Columbus. The great navigator is said to have first sailed into **Discovery Bay**, though he did not necessarily land here. As he found no fresh water, he named the place Puerto Seco, "dry harbour", then carried on westwards to the next horseshoe-shaped bay, at the mouth of the river he called **Rio Bueno**.

At the west side of Discovery Bay, on the cliff road to Montego Bay, and above the white-sand Puerto Seco beach lies the outdoor museum of **Columbus Park**. Just adjacent is the rust-red bauxite plant used in the filming of James Bond movie *Dr No*.

Along the coast are beautiful white sand beaches where you can practice kayaking and other water sports.

Falmouth and around

As well as its huge new cruise ship dock, the capital of the Trelawny parish has an admirable concentration of Georgian buildings. The town owed its prosperity to rum and sugar, as well as the slave trade, and was one of Jamaica's busiest ports in the late 18th and early 19th centuries. Its fortunes began to decline after 1840 and development halted, resulting in the preservation of its historic core. The Anglican **Church of St Peter** dates from 1796 and has a beautiful interior furnished with mahogany. At the side of **Water Square**, with its historic fountain, is the **Albert and George Market**; towards the harbour district, the **Phoenix Foundry** remains from an old ironworks. **Tharp House** on the waterfront was the home of one of the islands richest slave owners, while the nearby **Courthouse** is a grand old building fronted with a curved staircase and Doric columns. Just west, on Old Harbour Street, the **Barrett House** belonged to the great grandfather of English poet Elizabeth Barrett Browning.

Martha Brae

The popular rafting trip along this winding waterway begins, logically enough, in **Rafter's Village**, southwest of Falmouth, where you will find picnic facilities, souvenir shops, and refreshments.

Bamboo fringes the river as you drift through banana plantations, fields of sugar cane and yams. Small green parakeets, woodpeckers and the energetic bananaquit serenade you on your way. The journey ends at **Rock**, just west of Falmouth, where a bus awaits to bring visitors back to their hotels.

Mansions

On the coast west of Falmouth, **Greenwood Great House**, built in the 18th century, has fine furniture, early musical instruments.

Closer to Montego Bay, **Rose Hall** is said to be the home of the infamous "white witch", a restless young woman who killed all three of her husbands, as well as several miscellaneous lovers, and who is still said to haunt the rooms today. With its mahogany panelling, furniture in exotic woods and superb staircase, the mansion, built in 1760 and restored from a ruin, is one of the loveliest in Jamaica.

Montego Bay

MoBay, as it is familiarly called, entered the touristic scene early in the 20th century when a certain Dr McCatty, ahead of his time, advocated the bracing virtues of salt-water bathing. Nowadays nobody doubts the benefits, and Montego Bay has become part of Caribbean history. Most visitors spend their time on the Gloucester Avenue "Hip Strip", lined with restaurants, bars and hotels, which runs parallel to three spectacular beaches: Doctor's Cave, Cornwall and Walter Fletcher.

Montego Bay Town

The Cage, right in the centre of town on Sam Sharpe Square, dates from 1807. It used to be a jail for runaway slaves. On Sundays, the plantation slaves were allowed to come to town to sell their produce but they were supposed to leave after a bell rang at 2 o'clock. Any slaves still on the streets after the second bell at 3 were locked up in the Cage.

Also on Sam Sharpe Square, the **Old Court House** of 1804 has now been refurbished as the town's Civic Centre, with a small history museum. After the slave rebellion of 1831, this was the scene of hundreds of trials carried out in a summary fashion. Those found guilty—like one of their leaders Sam Sharpe himself— were strung up outside the courthouse to serve as examples.

The handsome Georgian **parish church of St James** was built at the end of the 18th century and faithfully reconstructed after an earthquake in 1957. Inside you'll see mahogany furnishings and two monuments by the British sculptor John Bacon (1740–99); outside are tropical gardens.

Jamaica's craft markets offer a wealth of local wares.

Down at the end of Market Street is the open-air **Craft Market**, where basketware, embroidery and wood-carving are featured.

Duty-free shops abound in Montego Bay, and at the designated complex at **Freeport**, on a small peninsula west of the city.

Inland from Montego Bay, near **Anchovy**, you can observe and photograph colourful birds such as the orange quit and doctor bird at **Rocklands Bird Sanctuary**. Mango hummingbirds fly down to drink from hand-held bottles. Feeding takes place around 4 p.m.

Cockpit Country

Inland is a landscape like something out of another world: huge potholes and sharp peaks carved out of the limestone, all covered with dense vegetation. This was one of the places where runaway slaves could hide out from the British, and their descendants still live in Maroon villages such as **Accompong**. The region is best visited on an organized trip from Montego Bay. You can also take a bus trip to the **Appleton Estate**, a plantation and rum distillery.

Negril

During the 1960s, the fishing village of Negril was discovered by hippies who visited to enjoy an offbeat, uncomplicated life "away from it all"; today, it's a fully fledged resort. On the way to this popular resort from Montego Bay, you pass through the pretty port of **Lucea**, which once handled sugar. It is overlooked by the crumbling Fort Charlotte, open for visits.

Negril is graced with a glorious stretch of white-sand beach, **Long Bay**, lapped by limpid clear waters and lined with bars, restaurants and hotels; around a headland to the north, **Bloody Bay** is equally lovely. Negril's **West End**, between South Negril River and the lighthouse, is especially attractive. The indentations in the rocky coastline make for good swimming and snorkelling.

THE HARD FACTS

Climate. Tropical all year. Temperate in mountain areas. The rainy months are May and October, but there can be rainfall at any time. Evenings tend to be cool. The hurricane season is from June to November.

Clothing. During the day shorts and beachwear are fine for the resorts and beaches, but to stroll in town you will need something dressier.

Communications. Falmouth cruise ship port is a wireless hotspot, though you have to pay a fee. There are Internet cafés in Montego Bay and Ocho Rios, and many bars and restaurants offer free wi-fi. You can make phone calls at the communications centres in all three of Jamaica's cruise ship terminals. Mobile phone roaming costs are high, so it's better to purchase a local SIM card if you plan to make a lot of calls.

Customs Allowance. Visitors aged minimum 18 may import the following goods duty-free: 200 cigarettes or 50 cigars or 225 g of tobacco; 1 litre of spirits (excluding rum); 1 litre wine; 150 g of perfume.

Driving. Traffic drives on the left. Big towns, and the airports, have car rental facilities; a consumption tax of 15 percent is imposed. A UK, US or Canadian driving licence is valid.

Electricity. The current is 110–120 volts, 50 Hz. Plugs have two flat pins; you will need an adapter.

Emergencies. For police, fire brigade and ambulance, call 112 or 911.

Money. The Jamaican dollar (J$ or JMD) is divided into 100 cents. Coins run from 25 cents to J$20, banknotes from J$50 to 1,000. The American dollar is also widely accepted. Credit cards are accepted almost everywhere, and there are exchange booths at all the cruise ports.

Time. UTC/GMT–5, all year round.

Transport. Privately run buses and minibuses cover destinations throughout the island; there are government-run services in Montego Bay and Kingston. Coach and taxi tours, often with JUTA, can be booked at most hotels. Taxis are unmetered, so agree on a fare before setting off.

Water. The tap water in hotels is filtered and chlorinated and is safe to drink. Bottled mineral water is widely available.

The gift of a smile from children in the
Dominican Republic.

hemis.fr / Rieger

Dominican Republic

The Dominican Republic occupies the eastern two-thirds of Hispaniola; the western part is French-speaking Haiti. The country's many beaches are fringed by two seas, the Caribbean and the Atlantic. We begin in the historic heart of the nation, the capital city that's better than ever after five centuries of development.

Santo Domingo

The capital city of Santo Domingo is crowned by many a superlative. Founded in 1496 by Columbus's brother Bartholomew, it is the oldest European-founded settlement in the western hemisphere. It also has the oldest cathedral in the New World, and its university was in the education business 78 years before Harvard.

Zona Colonial

The city proudly maintains its historic centre, or Zona Colonial. Restored and embellished for the 500th anniversary of the discovery of America, the old town was listed the same year (1990) by UNESCO as part of mankind's cultural heritage. Exploration of its cobbled lanes and shady squares, lined with charming colonial houses, Spanish palaces and ruined churches, is best done on foot; there are plenty of small cafés to take time off in between bouts of sightseeing.

Around the Cathedral

A visit to the historic heart of the capital starts at **Parque Colón**, in which stands a statue of Columbus, pointing to new horizons. Overlooking the park, the **Catedral Primada de America** was completed in the 1540s. The exterior is Renaissance, while the interior contains Gothic vaulting. The main entrance has a huge door weighing 2.5 tons. Guides point out the first chapel to the right of the altar where Francis Drake apparently slung his hammock in 1586 and broke off a statue's nose.

Southwest of the cathedral, the **Convento de los Dominicos** was the first building of the Dominican order in the Americas, and when it became the headquarters of the **Universidad Autónoma de Santo Domingo** in 1538, it was also the first university in the New World. The convent includes a church (1517) built on the groundplan of a Latin cross, a cloister, and the 1649 Capilla del Tercer Orden (Chapel of the Third Order).

East of the cathedral, overlooking the Ozama River, is the **Fortaleza Ozama**, the fortress begun in 1502 and completed a century later. It is dominated by the **Torre de Homenaje** (Tower of Homage). Built at the beginning of the 16th century, this square, no-nonsense edifice contains a wooden spiral staircase. Ships entering the harbour used to be saluted from here.

DOMINICAN REPUBLIC FLASHBACK

Early times
The island is inhabited by brown-skinned Tainos (meaning "the good ones"), related to the peaceful Arawak Indians of tropical South America.

15th century
On his first voyage to the New World, Christopher Columbus sights the island, which he names Hispaniola. He puts ashore a 40-man garrison near Cap Haïtien, but returning in 1493 he finds they had been wiped out. He founds a new colony, La Isabela, near the future Puerto Plata. In 1496 Columbus's brother Bartholomew establishes a permanent settlement on the south coast, Santo Domingo.

16th–18th centuries
Spanish conquests and exploitation of treasures in Mexico and Peru eclipse the importance of Santo Domingo. In an English offensive against the Caribbean, Sir Francis Drake sacks the city in 1586. France takes control of the western third of Hispaniola under the 1697 Treaty of Ryswick but Santo Domingo remains Spanish. In the 18th century African slaves are brought to Santo Domingo. After long-running border conflicts, France wins control of the entire island under the Treaty of Basel (1795).

19th century
Spain regains sovereignty in 1809. Santo Domingo attempts a revolution against Spain in 1821 but instead falls under Haitian rule. Dominicans rebel against Haiti in 1844, and independence is finally achieved. A US-style constitution is adopted.

20th century–present
Insurrections, assassinations and coups prompt the US to occupy the Dominican Republic (1916–24). Starting in 1930, the dictatorship of General Trujillo, his family and friends brings order—along with corruption and murderous civil rights abuses. Trujillo is assassinated in 1961. After several military coups, US Marines intervene (1965). The Dominican Republic celebrates the 500th anniversary of the Columbus voyage (1992), with tourism the prime source of foreign exchange. A modern metro system is inaugurated in Santo Domingo in 2008. Danilo Medina of the Dominican Liberation Party succeeds the first president Leonel Fernández in August 2012.

Calle Las Damas

The oldest street in the city, Calle Las Damas (Street of the Ladies), was named after the ladies-in-waiting of María de Toledo, Columbus' daughter-in-law. The cobbled street is lined with palaces, churches and colonial mansions. Cortés lived at the **Casa Hernán Cortés** at No. 42, now the French embassy; it was here that he prepared his expedition to Mexico.

The **Hostal Nicolás de Ovando** was the governor's palace at the beginning of the 16th century. The porch was designed in the Isabellan Gothic style, rarely seen on this continent. The building has been renovated and converted into a hotel boasting splendid courtyards, interior fountains and a terrace overlooking the river.

New World Landmarks

Set in the grand former Royal Court building, extensive material on pre-Columbian and colonial Dominican history fills the richly decorated rooms of the **Museo de las Casas Reales** (Royal Houses Museum). On the south side, the coat of arms of Queen Joan ("the Mad") is said to be the only one in the world commemorating her brief reign. The museum has excellent displays of colonial artefacts dating from 1492 to 1821 and includes pieces recovered from sunken Spanish galleons.

The **Alcázar de Colón** looms behind San Diego fort and gate, the former town entrance for anyone coming from the port. The rectangular, two-storey building is rather forbidding, despite a handsome façade underlined by ten stone arcades. It was built in 1509 by 1,500 Indians sentenced to hard labour, for Diego Columbus, his wife and court when he succeeded Nicolás de Ovando to the post of governor. It served as the seat of the viceroy for some 60 years, until Sir Francis Drake plundered it in 1586. Extensively restored, it now contains a museum of antiques, some of which belonged to the Columbus family. The rooms are decorated in a 16th-century style.

The **Casa del Cordón**, where Diego Columbus and his family lived until the Alcázar was completed, was the first stone building (1502) in colonial America. Currently the head office of a bank, it is decorated with a thick, sculpted rope, the symbol of the Franciscan order.

The colonial services of the arsenal and customs and excise were housed in the eight stocky buildings of the **Atarazana**, begun in 1507. Boutiques, galleries and restaurants have opened up for business in the little houses of the neighbouring streets, built on brick foundations and sporting intricate wrought-iron balconies.

The Alcázar is furnished in 16th-century style.

As night falls, the capital's riverside promenade, **Avenida del Puerto**, and its extension, the **Malecón**, turn into one vast party. This is the place to see, hear and join in the syncopated rhythms of the Dominican national dance, the *merengue*. The lighting effects are pure moonlight.

Faro a Colón

In **Parque Mirador del Este**, east of the Ozama River, the controversial Faro a Colón (Columbus Lighthouse) is a huge cross-shaped building, built for the 500th anniversary of the Columbus venture. Inside, a marble and bronze mausoleum contains the purported remains of the explorer. Lasers are used to project a crucifix of light into the sky, though are rarely turned on these days.

Parque Los Tres Ojos

East of the Faro a Colón, the Parque Nacional Los Tres Ojos holds an amazing coralline grotto, open to the skies, some 15 m deep. Amid tropical vegetation, stalactites and stalagmites, underground rivers have formed three lakes—the "eyes" of the park.

Modern Sights

Culture on a slightly higher plane is concentrated on the opposite side of the city in modern Santo Domingo. The **Plaza de la Cultura** is a showcase of modern art and architecture, grouping museums, the Biblioteca Nacional and the marble and mahogany **Teatro Nacional**. Contemporary sculptures are dotted around the square fronting the **Museo del Hombre Dominicano** (Museum of Dominican Man). The ground floor is devoted to Taíno culture; upstairs, displays cover folk traditions from the merriment of carnival to the horrors of slavery.

To the northwest, the **Museo Bellapart** (corner Av. J.F. Kennedy & Av. Dr Lembert Peguero) boasts a significant collection of local art.

DINING AND SHOPPING

On the menu

Among typical street snacks are *quipes* (various sandwiches), *pastelitos* (meat or fish patties) and *catibias* (stuffed manioc fritters). Rice, red beans and manioc, accompanied by boiled beef, pork or chicken, form the basis of local cooking. The *bandera dominicana*, or "Dominican flag" is a mixture of all these ingredients served as a stew garnished with fried plantains *(tostones)*. The national dish *sancocho* is a stew made of up to seven different meats, vegetables and beans, the whole generously flavoured with aromatic herbs. *Arroz con pollo*, chicken with rice, is prepared in a spicy Creole way. *Lechón asado* is roast pork. Fresh fish and seafood are often cooked with coconut milk or garlic and rosemary.

The favourite sweets are *dulces*, a sort of fudge made with goats' milk, flavoured with fruit or coconut.

The local beer, ice-cold, hits the spot on a hot day. Alternatively, tropical fruit juices are dependable refreshers. Dominican rum comes in several versions, from *blanco* (white), useful in mixed drinks, to *añejo*, specially aged to a sippably mellow state.

The best buys

Amber, the national gem, in colours from crystalline to dark brown, is skilfully worked into jewellery and small decorative objects. Larimar (Dominican turquoise) looks specially good set in silver. Local craftsmen produce ceramics and figurines, basketware, embroidery and leatherware. Clothing and shoes are Dominican specialities. Mahogany is carved into figurines, bowls and boxes. Smokers can stock up on the highly-prized Dominican cigars. Rum, too, makes a useful gift. Don't hesitate to ask for advice — or a tasting.

Dominican Republic Ministry Of Tourism

To the east on Calle Dr Delgado, the **Palacio Nacional** is a handsome symmetrical, neoclassical building topped by a dome. Built in the 1940s during Trujillo's dictatorship, it is still the seat of the government. You are allowed to visit inside, providing your legs are covered—no shorts.

Southeast of the palace lies the historic **Parque Independencia** (Independence Park).

East of Santo Domingo

Passengers arriving at Santo Domingo's **Las Americas International Airport** are only five minutes away from the shallow lagoon beaches of **Boca Chica**, a lively resort. This close to the city, the white sand beach is very popular, especially at weekends. Beyond, along the **Costa Caribe**, small but alluring resorts like **Juan Dolio** and **Guayacanes**.

At the heart of an important sugar-producing area, **San Pedro de Macorís** is known throughout the country for its university and (more importantly) for its baseball team—a sport which has become a local passion. The town was founded in 1820 by immigrants of several nationalities, all fleeing before the Haitian invasion. The town has several handsome buildings, such as the **Church of San Pedro Apóstol** in the English Gothic style, or the flashy fire station with its bright red walls.

La Romana

La Romana, surrounded by sugar cane fields, now is the centre of a big-time resort district. International superstars come to perform before 5,000 fans at the natural amphitheatre below a simulated 14th-century Italian village called **Altos de Chavón**. La Romana has its own international airport, which is handy for guests of the huge **Casa de Campo** resort complex, while postcard-perfect beaches here include **Bayahibe** and **Dominicus**.

Islands and Parks

Birdwatchers and others appreciate two offshore islands here—tranquil and tiny **Isla Catalina**, a stone's throw from la Romana, and **Isla Saona**, part of the **Parque Nacional del Este**, reputed for the variety of its flora and fauna, and for fantastic white-sand beaches such as **Puerto Laguna**.

Peninsula de Samaná

The Dominican Republic's newest cruise ship terminal is located at Samaná, north of Santo Domingo. The main attractions here are the beaches of tiny **Cayo Levantado**, the eerie limestone formations of the **Los Haitises National Park**, and the humpback whales that migrate through the DR's waters. You can go on whale-watching trips from Samana, which also has a **Whale Museum**.

THE HARD FACTS

Communications. In Santo Domingo there are Internet cafés along the Calle del Conde in the port of Don Diego and on the mezzanine level of the Sans Souci Terminal; Samaná also has many places offering Internet access. Cruise terminals and many restaurants and bars in the resorts offer wi-fi.

Electricity. The current is 110–120 volts, 60 Hz. Plugs have two flat pins; you will need an adapter. There are frequent power cuts, but hotels usually have their own generators to cope with such problems.

Emergencies. Dial 911 to call the police, fire service or an ambulance.

Money. The Dominican *peso* (RD$) is issued in coins from 1 to 25 pesos, and banknotes from 20 to 2000 pesos. US dollars are widely accepted. The best place to change money is in a bank – do not be tempted by the black market. The major credit cards are readily accepted in most hotels, restaurants and shops. Take note, also, of restrictions placed on currency imports and exports: amounts over 10,000 US dollars must be declared, and import and export of Dominican Pesos is restricted to under 20,000.

Telephone. The Dominican Republic is linked to the American telephone network, code 1 809. You can easily buy cards to use in payphones or a prepaid cellphone in any shopping centre, or a SIM card to use in your own phone. Note that roaming charges are high.

Time difference. UTC/GMT–4 all year round.

Tipping. Service charge is added to the restaurant bill along with tax, but an additional 5 to 10 percent tip is customary. Drivers of taxis and communal taxis *(públicos)* don't expect tips.

Transport. Santo Domingo has a modern metro running from San Domingo Norte to La Feria; you can buy a rechargeable Metro Card/Tarjeta Metrocard. Five more lines are planned. Local buses run to all destinations on the island. There are taxi ranks in most tourist areas. Taxis are unmetered, so agree on fares in advance.

Tourist Information. Santo Domingo's tourist information centre is on Calle Cayetano Germosen, esq. Avenida Gregorio Luperón.

Water. Most of the towns have safe water supplies, but it's wise to ask for bottled mineral water, especially in remote places.

The sunny and colourful Old Town of San Juan, officially called Municipio de la Ciudad Capital San Juan Bautista.

Huber/Kremer

Puerto Rico

Most visitors to Puerto Rico get no further than San Juan—especially the glitzy strip of hotel-lined beach that stretches from Isla Verde, past Condado (the "action" centre) to Old San Juan. You can count on the sun and fun, but while you're here, savour, too, the island's Spanish heritage. And if you have the opportunity you can make an excursion to the tropical rainforest, a banana plantation or the city of Ponce.

San Juan

While the island is bound at the south by the Caribbean Sea, this colourful harbour town overlooks the azure waters of the Atlantic Ocean. It has two main sections, the old and new town, and a magnificent beach that extends for several miles. Take time to wander around Old San Juan, the city's beautifully restored colonial section.

Old Town

You can take in the high spots of the old walled town in an intensive half-day tour. There is too much to cover in a single round, but you should not miss the formidable old forts, the late-Gothic churches and the Spanish-style plazas. During your visit you will also see unique balconied houses, wrought-iron grilles and arcaded patios.

Paseo de la Princesa

The 19th-century promenade, recently restored at great expense, leads west then north from the port, following the city wall.

Overlooking San Juan Bay, **La Fortaleza**—"the Fortress"—is a grand mansion built in 1540 to defend against the Carib Indians. As more advanced enemies appeared, the fort became too vulnerable; this was lucky for the island governors, who have lived and worked in the 40-room mansion for centuries. La Fortaleza has been listed as a UNESCO World Heritage Site since 1983, together with other national historic sites. You can tour the gardens, chapel and dungeons on weekdays.

The paseo passes the **Puerta de San Juan**, dating from the late 18th century and the oldest gate in the city wall. Visiting dignitaries used to land at this spot to be escorted in procession up to the cathedral via the pretty Caleta de San Juan.

Around the Cathedral

The **Cathedral of San Juan** (1529) was thoroughly rebuilt in the 19th century, having been twice damaged by hurricanes. The marble tomb near the transept on the left side holds the remains of Juan Ponce de León, the first governor.

El Convento Hotel opposite the cathedral is set in a former Carmelite convent, with the restaurant in the chapel. Nearby at

PUERTO RICO FLASHBACK

15th–16th centuries

The peaceful Taíno Indians welcome Christopher Columbus, accompanied by nobleman Juan Ponce de León, to their island of Borinquén on November 19, 1493. Columbus calls it San Juan. In 1508, Ponce de León founds a Spanish settlement, but its site proves to be unhealthy and indefensible. The colonists move to another bay, Puerto Rico ("Rich Port"). The two names are somehow exchanged. The Spaniards soon exhaust the island's gold and put the Indians to work growing sugar cane. Slaves are imported from West Africa and fortifications are built. Sir Francis Drake attacks the town in 1595, and is forced to retreat. The English fare better three years later when the Earl of Cumberland shrewdly outflanks and lays siege to the fortress of El Morro. The British take the fort but lose the island: they are routed by an epidemic of yellow fever and dysentery. San Juan has to be entirely rebuilt.

17th–18th centuries

The Dutch sail into the harbour and march into the deserted city. But El Morro refuses to surrender and the disgruntled Dutch depart after setting fire to San Juan. The Spaniards refortify, building a defensive wall around the town. The British make one more attempt in 1797, surrounding and blockading the city. Then suddenly the British withdraw—frightened, the legend goes, by a torchlight parade of praying women, which they mistake for Spanish reinforcements.

19th century

The repressive military rule of Spain is disturbed by a small insurrection in Puerto Rico in 1868. The insurgents are quickly suppressed but the weary Spanish decide to change their tactics and ease the tension. In 1872, slavery is abolished; in 1897, the island is granted autonomy. Eight months later, the United States, involved in the Spanish-American War, lands troops on the south coast and takes Puerto Rico.

20th century–present

Puerto Ricans are made US citizens in 1917 and given more say in internal affairs. Since 1952, Puerto Rico has been a self-governing Commonwealth, freely associated with the United States. The chance to become a US state was rejected in a referendum. One-third of all Puerto Ricans live in the US, which still leaves 4 million on the island.

255 Calle del Cristo, the **Casa del Libro**, in a handsome 18th-century building, offers displays on the history and design of books. During ongoing renovation works, part of the collection is displayed at 199 Callejón de la Capilla, though the original building is used for regular literary events.

From Plazoleta del Puerto, take **Calle Tetuán**, where you will see several Art Deco-style buildings.

Pastel-coloured buildings at sunset in Plaza de Armas.

Plaza de Armas

Hundreds of years ago, citizen-soldiers used to drill in Plaza de Armas, the central square of Old San Juan. Later it became a favourite meeting place. It has a grandstand, a fountain and several fast-food outlets. The **Alcaldía** (City Hall) was remodelled in the 1840s to resemble Madrid's equivalent, with arcades that seem to have been designed expressly for electoral speeches.

Plaza de San José

The statue of Juan Ponce de León was cast from British cannon, captured after an unsuccessful attack on San Juan in 1797. Ponce de León was buried in the church of **San José** until 1913, when he was moved to the cathedral. This all-white building was begun in 1532, and is a rare example of late-Gothic style brought to the New World. The great vaulted ceilings date from the 16th century.

Also on the plaza is the **Museo Pablo Casals**. Here you discover the memorabilia of the great Spanish cellist, who spent his last years in Puerto Rico. Exhibits include his favourite cello and film of Puerto Rico's annual Festival Casals (February–March).

There are more extensive displays at the square's **Museo de San Juan**, an orderly and fascinating rundown of Puerto Rico's history and culture, which also hosts a Saturday market in its pretty interior courtyard.

The **Convento de Los Dominicanos** once served as a refuge from the Carib Indians. More recently, it was the headquarters of the US Army's Antilles Command. Now the public can enjoy the tranquillity of its expansive, double-decker patio, a splendid example of Spanish colonial design, and visit the **Galería Nacional** which displays temporary exhibitions and works by Puerto Rican artists.

Plaza del Quinto Centenario

The "Quincentennial Plaza", a park and cultural complex, was inaugurated in 1992 on the 500th anniversary of Columbus's arrival in the New World. Its focal points are an exuberant fountain and a monumental granite totem pole, Totem Telurico.

The woodcarvers of Puerto Rico are famed for their *santos*, naïve religious figurines. An display of ancient pieces can be seen in the **Museo de las Americas**, on the first floor of the **Cuartel de Ballajá**, the former residential quarter for Spanish troops and their families. There are also collections of colonial and American Indian artworks.

Opposite, the former asylum for the poor now houses the **Instituto de Cultura Puertorriqueña**, which manages several museums promoting the culture and art of Puerto Rico.

Casa Blanca

The White House, a sprawling, Spanish-style structure of 1521, was the residence of the Ponce de León family for 250 years. It now houses a museum exhibiting various objects and furniture that illustrate life in the 16th and 17th centuries.

The prettiest route back down to the centre from Calle San Sebastián is the set of step streets. Tropical plants add to the charm.

Castillo San Felipe del Morro

At the peninsula's tip, El Morro is San Juan's most impressive fort. Look around at your leisure or join a guided tour. Service. You'll marvel at the engineering work that went into this self-contained, six-storey city. Walk down the tunnels, stairways, ramps and parade grounds; visit the ammunition stores, cannons, dungeons and kitchens. Often besieged, El Morro fell only once—to the British in 1598. To the west, across the channel into the city harbour, **Fort San Juan de la Cruz**, like El Morro, is UNESCO listed.

Around Plaza de Colón

The statue of Columbus on Plaza de Colón was erected in 1893, on the 400th anniversary of his discovery of Puerto Rico.

South of the square, **Teatro Tapia** (1832) was the social centre of 19th-century San Juan. It was restored in 1976 at about 300 times its original cost, the works financed by contributions plus a one-cent tax on every loaf of bread, and is now used to stage concerts and operas.

To the southwest, the 18th-century Casa del Callejón mansion (Callejón De La Capilla 319) displays antique chemists' equipment at the **Museo de Farmacia**, and exhibits on 19th-century San Juan at the **Casa de la Familia Puertorriqueña del Siglo XIX**.

Castillo de San Cristobal

A relatively modern element in San Juan's defence system, the Castillo de San Cristobal occupies a commanding clifftop position on the northeast flank of the Old San Juan headland. It was built between 1634 and 1783 and, as one of the largest and most impressive Spanish fortifications in the Americas, is listed as a World Heritage Site. Moats, ramps and tunnels link five separate structures with the main part of the fort looming far above the Atlantic. You can join a National Park Service tour or wander around on your own to explore the recreated soldiers' barracks, Plaza de Armas parade ground, gun turrets spiked with cannon and the Devil's Sentry Box, the oldest part of the fortification. Iguanas bask in the sun.

Isla Verde Beach and the metropolitan side of San Juan.

Metropolitan Area

The tourist track to and from the old city passes through the area called **Puerta de Tierra** (Land Gateway).

Just to the east begins the **Condado** section, the Miami Beach of Puerto Rico, where **Isla Verde Beach** has an offshore **Marine Reserve**. The white-sand **Condado Beach** is a popular swimming spot, with plenty of bars and restaurants, while the area's main shopping street, **Avenida Ashford**, is a great place for a browse.

Museums

Inland of Condado, the modern works in the **Museo de Arte Contemporáneao (MAC)** are housed in a stunning glass-roofed building. Just east, the **Museo de Arte de Puerto Rico** displays a huge collection. The surrounding **Santuce** area holds an arts centre and the **Plaza del Mercado de Santuce** market.

Casa Bacardi Visitor Centre

Across the bay to the west, get the lowdown on rum at the world's largest distillery, which can produce 100,000 gallons a day (or 21 million cases each year).

En la Isla

En la isla — "Out on the island" — is what Puerto Ricans call everything beyond metropolitan San Juan. Drive half an hour from the capital and you can find yourself in the utter wilderness of El Yunque and Luquillo Beach, often combined in one tour.

The rainforest of El Yunque shelters a stunning variety of flora and fauna.

El Yunque National Forest

As you'll soon discover, a tropical rainforest is just that: steaming hot, dripping wet, dense jungle. El Yunque (The Anvil), covers 11,300 ha and comprises a bird and wildlife sanctuary operated by the US Forest Service. More than 100 billion gallons of water drench these tangled slopes every year. There are several well-maintained hiking trails through the forest, ranging from a 15-minute stroll to a 2-hour trek up to the peak of El Yunque, at 1,065 m. The **El Portal Rain Forest Center** has some excellent exhibits on the park's ecosystems.

About 240 species of trees grow here, 23 of them indigenous, and 150 tree ferns. There are several kinds of forest, depending on the altitude: the lower zones are dominated by rubber trees *(tabonuco)*, with higher up the stout, gnarled *palos colorados*, towering Sierra palms and dwarf trees. Seek out tiny orchids and listen for the song of the little *coquí* frog, Puerto Rico's unofficial emblem.

Luquillo

Near the turnoff for El Yunque, and overlooked by the Sierra Luquillo hills, Luquillo beach is a lovely curve of sand, framed by swaying coconut palms and known for its colourful snack kiosks *(friquitines)*.

Fajardo

In the northeastern part of the island, Fajardo has a huge marina, **Puerto del Rey**, and several beaches with calm, clear waters. The nearby **Las Cabezas de San Juan** headlands form a natural reserve of coral reefs, lagoons, mangroves and forest, accessible only by booking an organized tour. Ferries go several times a day to the peaceful islands of **Vieques** and **Culebra**, renowned for their superb beaches and their reefs. At Vieques, Bioluminescent Bay is the most beautiful of the three areas in Puerto Rico illuminated at night by microorganisms that glow neon-blue when the water is disturbed.

Ponce

Also known as the Pearl of the South, Ponce is Puerto Rico's second city, a gem of preserved 19th-century colonial architecture centreing on the stately cathedral of Our Lady of Guadalupe, on **Plaza Las Delicias**, with its lion fountain and gaudy black-and-red **Parque de Bombas** fire station. Near the plaza, the **Museo de la Historia de Ponce** is devoted to the town's history and culture. Further south, the newly renovated **Museo de Arte** (2325 Avenida Las Américas) holds a magnificent collection of European and American art from the 3rd century BC to the present day.

DINING AND SHOPPING

On the menu

Flavoured with two distinctly creole *(criollo)* seasonings— *sofrito* and *adobo*—the food tends to be mildly spicy with overtones of garlic, oregano and coriander. For your first course, black bean soup *(sopa de habichuelas negras)* can be superb. Nothing is more typically Puerto Rican than *asopao*, a rice stew with chicken, seafood or pigeon peas. There are lots of other good rice dishes to choose from, such as *paella* and *arroz con pollo* or "simple" rice and beans. *Pescado* means fresh fish. Try the red snapper *(chillo)*, hake *(merluza)* or sea bass *(mero)*.

If you have room left for dessert, pass over the staple puddings for the intriguing *dulce de lechosa con queso blanco,* papaya cubes cooked in sugar and cinnamon with white cheese; or perhaps *arroz con dulce*, boiled rice in coconut cream, sugar and cinnamon.

There are dozens of colourful rum concoctions to sample. Local daiquiri flavours include banana and coconut.

The best buys

Handicrafts include papier-mâché fruit and vegetables that look almost good enough to eat. For something particular to the island, consider buying a set of *santos*: these hand-carved wooden figures of saints originated in the 16th century. Straw hats, like the *pava*, an upswept model worn by farmers *en la isla*, are available full-sized or in a miniature version. You'll find chic resort wear, especially for women. Hand-screened textiles in novel designs are a growing industry on the island. Jewellery varies from inexpensive mother-of-pearl pieces to 18-carat creations by skilled artisans. Puerto Rican tobacco is one of the ingredients in hand-rolled cigars. The workers smoke them all day long, so they must be good.

Centro Ceremonial Indígena de Tibes

This pre-Columbian village north of Ponce was discovered in 1975 after Hurricane Eloise uncovered pieces of shell, ceramics and a cemetery. Tours take in a small museum and courts for playing the Taino ball-game, *batey*.

Hacienda Buena Vista

Inland of Ponce, this sprawling coffee plantation is still in operation as a working estate. It offers a great insight into colonial Puerto Rico. You can tour the restored great house, decked out with period furnishings, and see the water turbine and former slave quarters.

San Germán

In the southwest, the island's second-oldest city, founded in 1511, is a peaceful, picturesque town that has retained its Spanish colonial atmosphere. On Plaza San Domingo, the Gothic-style **Porta Coeli Church** (Gate of Heaven) dates from 1606, when it was built by Dominican monks. It has been restored to serve as a **Museum of Religious Art**, including Mexican colonial paintings and wood statuary of the 18th and 19th centuries.

Nearby beaches include **Phosphorescent Bay** and the delightful **Boquerón**, great for swimming. The village is also home to the **Refugio de Aves de Boquerón**, where paths through the mangrove swamps allow you to get up close to the 60 bird species which live there.

Mayagüez

Mayagüez stands at one end of the **Panoramic Route** which runs the whole length of the island, through the Cordillera Central all the way to Yabucoa. Its narrow roads meander through forest reserves and green valleys, offering magnificent views. The town is home to the **Parque Zoological Dr Juan A. Riviero**, where the resident animals include lions, tigers, elephants and gorillas.

Isla Mona

The "Galapagos of the Caribbean", tiny Mona is a 3-hour boat ride from the mainland. Taíno Indians lived here, then pirates and privateers, but its 57 sq km (22 sq miles) are now left to the wildlife: giant iguanas, hawksbill and leatherback turtles, red-footed boobies and other seabirds. No more than 100 visitors are allowed at a time.

Rincón

At the westernmost point of the island, the mountains run down to the sea, and the lovely beaches are popular with Puerto Rican families and American surfers in winter. Humpback

whales visit these waters in the same season, and platforms for spotting whales and dolphins have been built near the lighthouse at **Punta Higüero**.

Río Camuy

More than a million years ago, the Camuy River carved out great subterranean caverns from the limestone of this jagged karst region, a paradise for spelunkers. **Río Camuy Cave Park** has civilized the whole area, with picnic areas, walking trails and exhibition hall. Safe viewing of the underground world is organized at **Cueva Clara**, where visitors ride a sort of tram into a cavern to admire the impressive formations of stalactites and stalagmites.

Centro Ceremonial Indígena Caguana

Deep in the lush central forests near Utado, this former Taíno site was used for ceremonial purposes. Surrounded by granite slabs decorated with petroglyphs, excavations have revealed several *bateyes* or ball courts, while a museum displays the many precious artefacts uncovered here.

Batey court, petroglyphs and monoliths at the Centro Ceremonial Indígena Caguana. | A cocky little coquí in the rainforest.

THE HARD FACTS

Clothing. Away from the beach, Puerto Rico is fairly conservative, but shorts are acceptable in most public places. At night, people tend to dress up, especially in the casinos and nightclubs, and jackets are often required for men in smart restaurants.

Communications. Puerto Rico is part of the US network. The area code is 1 787, and the international access code is 011. Most hotels have wi-fi, and you will find Internet cafés in the cities. There is also free wi-fi access at the many chain restaurants.

Customs Allowance. Visitors of 21 years or older may import, duty-free: 200 cigarettes or 50 cigars or 2 kg (4.4 lb) tobacco and 1 quart of alcoholic beverages.

Driving. Traffic drives on the right. Car hire is available from international operators at the airport and at city agencies at very reasonable prices. Take care on the winding roads.

Emergencies. For fire, police or ambulance services, call 911.

Language. The two official languages are Spanish and English, but only a quarter of the islanders speak English well.

Money. The US dollar is the official currency. Major credit cards are widely accepted, and there are ATMs in all towns.

Tourist Information. The Puerto Rico Tourism Company has offices in the San Juan cruise port and on the Paseo de la Princessa.

Transport. If you don't want to hire a car you can make use of the local minibus services *(guaguas* or *públicos),* which are more like collective taxis. They link the capital to the main towns, but they stop in the late evening and do not run on Sundays. White taxis called Taxis Turistico can be hailed in the street or called by phone; they are equipped with meters, though the usual tourist routes have fixed tariffs. Expect to add a tip of 15%. Several local air companies have regular flights to the islands of Vieques and Culebra, and also Ponce and Mayagüez. The islands are also served by car ferries and express ferries that shuttle back and forth three or four times a day.

Water. Tap water is purified and considered safe to drink but you may prefer bottled mineral water. Do not swim or paddle in rivers and streams.

A cluster of rocks forms a dramatic background to The Baths, a famous cove on Virgin Gorda.

LESSER ANTILLES

This extended arc of islands, which sweeps from the east of Puerto Rico down to the coast of Venezuela, haphazardly defines where the Atlantic ends and the Caribbean begins. Some of them have been grouped according to both their geographical situation, running from north to south, as well as considering the different countries to which they belong. Most of them are tiny and inhabited only by colonies of birds, and the majority are verdant and volcanic. From the British and US Virgin Islands to the ABC Islands, these lush fragments of paradise are perfect for getting away from it all.

British Virgin Islands

Few people can tell you for sure how many islands make up the British Virgins—it all depends on the tide. There are around 60 islands and cays, of which 16 are inhabited. Mostly of volcanic origin, these tiny and relatively undeveloped islands, known locally as thee BVI, are a sleepy relic of an empire. British rule rests lightly on the 29,000 inhabitants, whose dignity and independent outlook stem from a long tradition of land ownership. Mostly, they will greet you with overwhelming charm—even if their English dialect might baffle you at first.

Tortola
Almost 80 percent of the population lives on Tortola, the largest and the best-known of the British Virgin Islands. The name is Spanish for turtledove.

Road Town
The capital of the BVI has no pretensions. Main Street winds through town, and a waterfront drive connects the old town to **Wickhams Cay**. Many banks and other financial institutions are located on this land which was formerly a burial ground for slaves. As befits any colonial capital, Road Town also has a Government House and Legislative Assembly building.

BRITISH VIRGINS FLASHBACK

Pre-Columbian era

The first known settlers of the islands are the Ciboney Indians from the South American mainland. They are followed by the Arawak Indians who in turn succumb to the warlike Caribs.

15th–16th centuries

Columbus meets a hostile reception when he tries to land on the islands during his second voyage in 1493. He names them Las Once Mil Vírgines and claims them for Spain. Spanish slave-hunters and pirates wipe out the Indians.

17th century

Dutch buccaneers build a settlement and fort on Tortola in 1648. The British seize Tortola and annex the islands in 1672. Colonists establish cotton, sugar and indigo plantations on Tortola and Virgin Gorda.

18th–19th centuries

The first half of the 18th century sees increasing prosperity and the arrival of missionaries—notably Quakers. The seat of government is transferred from Virgin Gorda to Tortola in 1741, and in 1774 the first elected assembly meets. The American War of Independence marks the start of economic decline. By the end of the century, law and order are reported to have broken down. The Napoleonic Wars bring British war-ships to Road Harbour, which becomes a free port, but the economic decline is accelerated by drought and a disastrous hurricane. The islands become part of the Leeward Island Federation in 1816. In 1834, the islands' 5,000 slaves are freed. A revolt breaks out in 1853, and cholera sweeps the islands. Plantations are abandoned and the islands revert to bush.

20th century–present

The colonial government makes an attempt to revive agriculture, but two hurricanes in 1916 and 1924 spell economic setback. The British Virgin Islands become a separate colony in 1956. A constitution in 1967 gives the islands a ministerial system of government and they are now largely self-governing, with the Premier as head of government as decreed by a new constitution in 2007. Tourism and offshore banking emerge as the islands' major industries.

British Virgin Islands

Caribbean Sea

Atlantic Ocean

Sir Francis Drake Channel

Anegada

The Settlement
Cooper Rock
Salt Pond
East End Point
White Point
Pearl Point
Deep Bay
Lobolly Bay
Cow Wreck Bay
Windlass Bight
Bone Bay
Soldier Point
Bird Sanctuary
Flamingo Pond
Set Bay
West End Point
Pomato Point
Spanish Town
Setting Point
Lower Bay

Virgin Gorda
Necker Island
Eustatia Island
Deep Bay
Prickly Pear Island
Berchers Bay
Mosquito Island
North Sound
Gun Creek
Virgin Gorda National Park
417 m Gorda Peak
South Sound Bluff
Savannah Bay
Handsome Bay
Spanish Town
Little Dix Bay
Virgin Gorda Airport
Copper Mine Point
Copper Mine N.P.
Spring Bay N.P.
The Baths
Devil's Bay N.P.
Collison Point
St Thomas Bay
Fallen Jerusalem
Round Rock
Ginger Island
Cooper Island

Anegada Setting Point (33 km)
Mountain Pt
Gorda Peak
George Dog
Great Dog
West Dog
Scrub Island
Cam Bay
Trellis Bay
Beef Island
The Bluff
Buck Island
Whelk Point
Dead Chest
Salt Island
Great Harbour
Peter Island
White Bay
Peter I. Bluff
Norman Island
Money Bay
Treasure Point
Pelican Island
Flanagan Passage
Privateer Point
Flanagan Island

Tortola
Great Camanoe Island
Guana Island
White Bay
Josiah's Bay
Brewer's Bay
Shark Bay
Terrance B. Lettsome International Airport
Long Swamp
Hog's East Long Bay
Bluff Bay
Long Look
Josiah's Hill
Turnbull
Mount Healthy National Park
Brandywine Brothers
Wesley Will
Belle Vue
Mt Sage 385 m
Road Town
Baughers Bay
Cane Garden Bay
Brierdiff-Davis Observatory
Soldier's Hill
Sandy Cay
Callwood Rum Distillery
Long Bay
Carrot Bay
Sage Mt.
542 m
Sage Mt N.P.
Freshwater Pond
Hannah
Cow Bay
Sea Cow Bay
Havers
Allwood Rum Distillery
Dolphin Discovery
Fort Recovery
Slaney
West End
Sopers Hole
Frenchman's Cay
Smuggler's Cove
Belmont Bay

Great Thatch Island

Jost Van Dyke
Diamond Cay National Park
Great Harbour
White Bay
Little Jost Van Cay
Little Green Cay
Garner Harbour

St John (USA)
Annaberg Ruins
Coral Bay
Maho Bay
Palestina
Calabash Boom
East End

Settling Point
Spanish Town

0   5 km

N

The tiny **Virgin Islands Folk Museum** on Main Street displays artefacts from the plantation and slavery eras alongside Arawak finds and salvage from local shipwrecks. There is more local history at the quaint **Old Government Museum** on Waterfront Drive, beautifully furnished in period style.Just northwest, you can cool off in the shade of the **J.R. O'Neal Botanical Gardens**.

Island Sights

Just outside Road Town, you can swim with dolphins at **Dolphin Discovery**. Tortola's best bathing spots are on the north coast. At **Cane Garden Bay**, the gorgeous beach slopes from leaning palm trees into the sea. Just behind, the **Callwood Rum Distillery** offers insight into this age-old local industry. Tours include a tasting and a look at the grand 200-year-old copper boiling vat. At Carrot Bay further down the coast, the quirky **North Shore Shell Museum** displays not only treasures from the sea but also wooden boats and other crafts.

Inland Tortola

Scenery is the high point of a tour of Tortola. The top of **Joe's Hill**, on the western side of Road Town, gives you a bird's-eye view of Road Harbour. **Soldier's Hill** affords the fine panorama of Brewer's Bay, where forested hills enclose a superb snorkelling and bathing beach. Above the bay, **Mount Healthy National Park** offers views, picnic spots and a ruined windmill that once turned on an 18th-century sugar plantation.

At the West End of the island, **Soper's Hole Wharf & Marina** is a charming anchorage with lots of shops, restaurants, bars and entertainment. Ferries run from here to Jost Van Dyke and St Thomas in the US Virgins. Attractive terraced villas dot the hillsides.

Walk or ride to the top of 542-m **Mount Sage** to see what the island looked like before slaves cleared it for cane. A national park preserves the remains of the lush forest.

Virgin Gorda

The half-hour ferry ride affords spectacular views of Tortola's undeveloped coastline and of the islands west of Virgin Gorda. The third-largest of the British Virgin Islands, only 4,000 people live here, although it was once a thriving commercial centre.

Spanish Town

Virgin Gorda's capital (also known as The Valley) is a quaint settlement with shops, restaurants and tiny hotels. South of the yacht harbour, stone walls remain from an old Spanish fort in the **Little Fort National Park**, and on the island's southwest tip, at the **Copper Mine**

National Park, you can see relics of a copper mine worked by Cornish miners in the middle of the 19th century. But Virgin Gorda is best known for **The Baths**, about a mile down Millionaire's Road from Spanish Town. It's as if a giant hand has flung huge, house-sized granite boulders across the white sand of a cove. The sea rushes in to form a labyrinth of crystal-clear channels and pools, which shimmer in the reflected light.

Other Islands

To the southwest of Virgin Gorda stretches a string of cays.

Peter Island

Directly opposite Road Town across the Sir Francis Drake Channel, Peter Island is a luxurious, privately owned resort. The port is **Sprat Bay**, popular with yachtsmen from around the world. The sweeping crescent of **Deadman's Bay** is rated as one of the world's most romantic beaches, and there are 30 dive sites, notably Carrot Shoal and Shark Point.

Norman Island

It is said to be Robert Louis Stevenson's Treasure Island. You'll enjoy snorkelling and exploring the sea caves at **Treasure Point**, and having drinks or dinner at the two beach restaurants. Close by is the rocky Dead Chest Island, celebrated in the song "Fifteen men on a dead man's chest, yo-ho-ho and a bottle of rum". It's an uninhabited national park with three dive sites, including the **Painted Walls**: vertical rock faces encrusted with brightly coloured sponges and cup corals.

Salt Island

Beyond Dead Chest, this island used to provide the English monarch with an annual sack of salt from its ponds. Divers come to explore the extensive wreck of *RMS Rhone*, a transatlantic Royal Mail steamer smashed against a reef by a hurricane in 1867. It's now a renowned dive site, encrusted with coral and home to all kinds of sealife.

Just Van Dyke

Northwest of Tortola, Jost Van Dyke is a tiny, luxuriant paradise hemmed with white sand. **Great Harbour** is a pretty village of wooden houses that seems lost in time. While you're here, drop in at the infamous Foxy's bar for a cocktail and a bite to eat. Close to town, stunning **White Bay Beach** is the best on the island.

Anegada

As far away from it all as you can get, limestone and coral Anegada, offers infinite white-sand beaches and stark salt ponds inhabited by flamingos. Have a lobster meal in the main town, **The Settlement**.

DINING AND SHOPPING

On the menu

For starters, conch fritters or *escabeche*, pickled fish served cold, could well be on the menu. Or try *gundy*, a spread featuring salt cod or lobster mashed with onions, olives and peppers. The soup made from papaya is delicious, too. For the main course, you may want to order conch. It's excellent cooked the French way, sautéed in garlicky butter with herbs. Among the most favoured island fish are red snapper, kingfish, bonito, tuna and the local fish known as dolphin (not the porpoise). Fish is often served with Johnny Cakes, fried flour dumplings that are delicious when served piping hot, uninspiring when cold.

No main dish is more typically West Indian than *callaloo*. This fragrant stew normally contains at least pork, fish, crab or conch, plus okra, spinach or other greens, onions and garlic. You may want to accompany your meal with a fruit drink or rum cocktail rather than expensive imported wines. Beer is reasonably priced and tasty.

The best buys

Macramé, the sailor's art, still flourishes here. Scrimshaw is practised in the form of engravings on bone or seashells. Necklaces, bracelets and pendants can be made of seeds, shells or pottery. Island mothers have traditionally made rope dolls for their children. A *mocko jumbie* doll, with magic overtones, comes dressed as a clown. Philatelists prize the British Virgin Islands stamps.

The whole area of the US Virgins is duty-free. In St Thomas you can buy gemstones such as larimar, the colour of the sea.

flickr.com/joyosity

US Virgin Islands

The majority of Virgin Islanders are descendants of African slaves who laboured for European plantation owners until emancipation in the mid-19th century. More and more of the population, however, is not native-born: "down islanders" from elsewhere in the Caribbean, as well as Puerto Ricans and mainland Americans, have been moving in to these still sparsely inhabited islands, particularly St Thomas and St Croix. The resulting ethnic and cultural blend is intriguing, and unusually harmonious.

St Thomas

The busiest and best-known of the Virgin Islands is St Thomas, which enjoys its reputation of being a shoppers' paradise. But retail therapy is only one of its many pleasures: it's well worth getting out and exploring the island, with its dramatic wooded hills, intimate beaches, historic houses and inspiring seascapes. The capital and only city of St Thomas is the prettily named Charlotte Amalie, honouring the consort of Christian V, king of Denmark in the 17th century. Most of the island's population lives in the town, which rises steeply and majestically from the port district. The port is the starting and finishing point for many cruises; there is always a line of ships at the quayside.

Charlotte Amalie

The Virgin Islands' 15-member Senate occupies the stately **Legislature Building** just beyond the Coast Guard headquarters at King's Wharf. It was built over a century ago to house Danish police, and is where the Danish flag was lowered for the last time when the US formally took possession of the Virgin Islands in 1917.

Around the Fort

Across the road, a solid chunk of history, **Fort Christian**, is embodied in an aloof fortress with the date 1671 on its façade. Due to restoration works, the fortress is closed to the public for an indefinite period; however, you can walk around the exterior.

Between the fort and the post office, the **Emancipation Garden** commemorates the proclamation of the abolition of slavery in 1848 by the governor Peter von Scholten. The big bell at the southwest corner of the park is a replica of the iconic Liberty Bell in Philadelphia.

Frederick Lutheran Church, thought to be the island's oldest, was built in 1826 an older church destroyed in a fire. A wide staircase leads to an imposing entrance. Further east along the same street (Norre Gade), the **Moravian Memorial Church**, with its fine wooden cupola, dates from 1882.

US VIRGINS FLASHBACK

15th–16th centuries
After Columbus claims the islands for Spain, the Indian inhabitants are forced into slavery. The islands become the haunt of pirates.

17th century
In 1625, English and Dutch settlers establish rival outposts on St Croix. After 20 years of bloody struggle, the English prevail, but they are expelled by Spanish forces in 1650, who themselves surrender to the French in the same year. St Croix is bequeathed in 1653 to the Knights of Malta, who sell out to the French West India Company 12 years later. In 1657 Dutch settlers establish a colony on St Thomas but soon abandon the island. A contingent of Danes and Norwegians found the settlement of Charlotte Amalie in 1672.

18th century
Danish settlers from St Thomas cross to St John in 1717, establishing plantations of cotton and tobacco. St Thomas is declared a free port in 1724. A slave uprising on St John in 1733 gives the slaves a free community for six months. Forces are brought in to quell the rebellion and all the slaves die, many committing suicide at Mary's Point. The same year, France sells St Croix to the Danish West India Company. Denmark names St Thomas a crown colony in 1734.

19th century
St Thomas and St John change hands several times while the English and the Danes struggle to establish supremacy. The economy of St Thomas declines in the 1820s with a slump in cane sugar prices and the advent of the steamship. Governor von Scholten frees the slaves of the Danish islands in 1848. Cholera epidemics sweep the Virgins. Riots break out and sugar production all but ceases.

20th century–present
During World War I, the US buys St Thomas and St John, with St Croix and some 50 islets and outcrops for $25 million. Islanders are granted voting rights in 1936. They gain greater independence in 1954 with the creation of a three-branch central government, headed since 1970 by an elected governor. Tourism becomes a main pillar of the economy.

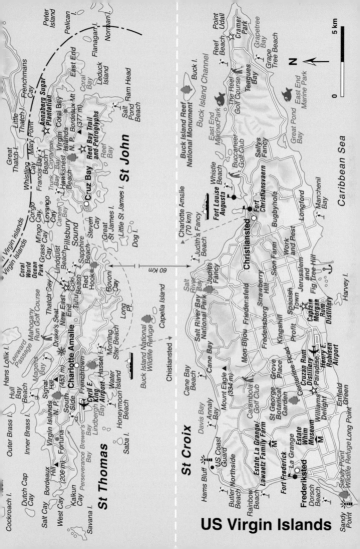

Government House, a gracious, three-storey brick edifice with long wrought-iron balconies, was built by the Danish rulers in 1867. It serves as the office of Virgin Islands' elected governor.

The higher you climb in St Thomas the more thrilling the views; as exploited by well-to-do 18th-century colonists, who built their houses on hilltops overlooking the harbour. The hills were too steep for roads, so stone staircases were built as step-streets. The most famous is called the **99 Steps**, at the top of which is **Blackbeard's Castle** or Skytsborg, a stone tower with a superb view. It was the haunt of a legendary 18th-century buccaneer, Bristol-born Edward Teach.

The **Beracha Veshalom Vegimulth Hasidim Synagogue** (also known as St Thomas Synagogue) was rebuilt in 1833 on the site of several previous Jewish temples dating back to the 11th century — making it the second-oldest synagogue in the United States, and the oldest in continuous use. A French architect laid out its traditional design, with three sides of benches facing inward.

Shopping District

Downhill from the synagogue, the shopping district concentrated on or near Main Street (still officially known by its Danish name, **Dronningens Gade**) is a shopper's dream come true. Few streets in the world sell so many luxurious goods so temptingly displayed. Also on Main Street is the **Pissarro Building**, childhood home of the famous artist. A small gallery displays a couple of his sketches.

Main Street becomes less glamorous — but no less fascinating — at **Market Square**, where islanders buy and sell local fruits and vegetables, from frangrant mangoes and papaya to earth-covered tubers of yam and cassava.

You can take a break from the heat at **Magic Ice**, a super-cool attraction dedicated to all things frozen, from ice sculptures to slides.

Bluebeard's Castle

A short way to the east, this round stone tower of brick and rubble masonry was built by the Danish government in 1678 as a coast defence installation. Its 11 cannon were manned until 1735. According to local legend, The pirate used this tower as a lookout, lair and love-nest. One version recounts that the villain discovered his bride there with another man; he slew her and sailed away, never to be heard of again. In fact, no official record of Bluebeard's tenancy exists, but the myth adds a piquant touch to what is now the honeymoon suite of a luxury hotel, built around the tower in 1933.

Havensight Mall

The large, modern **Havensight Mall** next to the cruise ship dock has some 60 shops and is surrounded by smaller scale malls. From here, the **St Thomas Skyride** cable-car whisks you up the mountain-side to **Paradise Point** for a sweeping view of the harbour.

Frenchtown

Almost attached to Hassel Island, the area acquired its name from the French-speaking settlers who came from St Barthélemy in the mid-19th century. They have retained their ancient Norman dialect—and their fishing skills.

Hassel Island

The narrow, shallow isthmus that once linked Hassel Island to the "mainland" was replaced by a major channel, dredged after the United States bought the Virgins in order to provide an alternative escape route for the American fleet should the harbour be attacked. Now part of the **Virgin Islands National Park**, the island's landmarks include a 19th-century mountaintop signal tower.

Brewer's Bay

The charming white-sand beach is owned by the University of the Virgin Islands but open to the public. The college itself occupies 70 ha (175 acres) of attractively landscaped hillsides.

Mountain Top

Head up 460 m to enjoy a magnificent view down onto Magens Bay and out to an array of US off-islands and the British Virgins; and to sample a banana daiquiri, invented at a hotel which once stood here.

Drake's Seat

Legend has it that this was the spot from which the British Admiral Sir Francis Drake surveyed the fleet he assembled in 1595 to attack Puerto Rico. This most famous of Elizabethan admirals had already captured many Spanish bastions, but this time his the tactics failed to match the firepower of San Juan's El Morro fortress. Embittered and feverish, the navigator died of dysentery soon after this defeat, and was buried at sea.

Blackbeard The Buccaneer.
Edward Teach is said to have accumulated 14 wives, though it's uncertain whether they were wed consecutively or rather deployed concurrently on various islands. The scandalous career of this giant among scoundrels ended in a shoot-out with the British navy in 1718. Blackbeard's tower achieved sudden respectability in 1831 when it was converted to an astronomical observatory.

Beaches

Magens Bay is the island's biggest and most flawless beach. unspoiled thanks to government conservation efforts, this palm-backed stretch of sand really is one of the most glorious beaches in the world. Arthur S. Fairchild, an American publishing tycoon, gave the property to the people of the Virgin Islands in 1946.

More spectacular beaches are just downhill from the Smith Bay road heading to the east end of the island. At **Coki Beach**, **Coral World Ocean Park** has an undersea observatory featuring a walkway into a coral reef. The aquariums are home to an array of sea life, and you can explore the nature trails, feed the stingrays and birds, touch baby sharks and starfish and swim with sea lions. Coki is rated best local beach for snorkelling. Luxury hotels and condominiums snuggle on secluded coves with names as appealing as Pineapple Beach, Pelican Bay and Sapphire Beach.

St John

On the smallest and most beautiful of the three major American islands, nature reigns supreme. Human intrusion is minimal, and the result is the envy of the Caribbean. Encircled by beaches of powdery white coral sand , some forty coves enclose a hundred hues of blue and green. Behind them are coconut groves and then tangled forests with ruins of old Danish plantations. Flowers, ferns and butterflies abound.

St John owes its unspoiled tranquillity to the fact that 56 percent of its rugged landscape and most of its offshore waters are preserved as the **Virgin Islands National Park**. This park has existed since 1956 on acreage donated by Laurance Rockefeller, but it has since been extended to incorporate Hassel Island on St Thomas. There are more than 20 hiking trails, along with guided tours, historic programmes and some spectacularly ornate and pristine reefs to explore. Be sure to pick up maps and information at the **Cruz Bay Visitor Center**, on the north side of the harbour.

Cruz Bay

The sleepy capital of St John is so tiny that no one has even bothered to name its streets. The harbour, also called Cruz Bay, is used by yachts and ferries from St Thomas. Modern life has made some inroads, such as the shopping malls of Mongoose Junction and Wharfside Village.

Centerline Road climbs up around the tallest peak, Bordeaux Mountain; at almost 400 m, it offers breathtaking views of the Atlantic, Caribbean and nearby islands. You'll see down to remote Mary's Point on the north shore where St John's slave rebellion of 1733 ended tragically. It's also known as Suicide Point.

From another lookout (weather permitting) you can see across to St Croix, 65 km (40 miles) away.

From **Coral Bay Overlook**, no less than eleven of the neighbouring British Virgin Islands lining the channel named for Sir Francis Drake make a photograph to remember. From here you can gaze down on **St John's Hurricane Hole**, a protected bay where sailors have fled storms over the centuries. This panorama is considered by many to be the best in the Caribbean.

Towering above the picturesque north shore ruins of the **Annaberg** sugar and rum factory is a 150-year-old windmill, one of the largest in the Virgin Islands.

Beaches

No picture book can prepare you for the glorious beaches strung one after another along St John's reef-fringed northwestern shore.

Trunk Bay may well be the most perfect of perfect beaches. The snorkelling trail in the emerald water is well used and partially damaged but remains ideal for novices. Its sunken symbols and signs are clearly visible at a maximum depth of 4 m.

Whenever Greta Garbo wanted to be alone, she checked in to **Caneel Bay**, a resort founded by Lau-

Françoise Ohayon

With its white sand, turquoise seas and swaying palms, Trunk Bay on St John is a picture-perfect beach.

rance Rockefeller. Celebrities, politicians and industrialists appreciate its gentle beaches and unobtrusive luxury. Ordinary mortals may stroll the grounds, examine the beaches, buy a drink or have lunch. There are some interesting old sugar buildings.

St Croix

Long, leisurely and lovely, St Croix lies in the Caribbean some 64 km (40 miles) south of the other Virgin Islands. The name is pronounced Saint Croy; it means "Holy Cross". You'll soon appreciate that this is a very special tropical island. The unhurried Crucians number about 55,000 and live on St Croix's 212 sq km (82 sq miles) of rolling countryside and satellite isles. That makes it by far the largest of the Virgins, but boasting is not the style. There are only two towns, Frederiksted and Christiansted.

Frederiksted

Fronting on the tranquil west-coast sea, Frederiksted wears a sleepy look, and its few modern buildings don't even begin to disturb the old-fashioned, world-passed-by atmosphere. A vital feature is the pier put up in 1994 to accommodate multiple cruise ships; it's a popular snorkelling spot when no boats are in dock.

Fort Frederik, now restored, stands near the pier; it was built in the mid-18th century, primarily to discourage smuggling which flourished from the west end of St Croix. It was at this fort that harried Governor von Scholten declared, in an explosive situation in 1848: "All unfree in the Danish West Indies are from today free". A small museum gives some background on the Emancipation.

Overlooking the waterfront on Strand Street, the **Caribbean Museum Center for the Arts** has changing displays of work from the various local artists in residence, and special events such as live music and Latin dance.

Strolling Frederiksted's esplanade and downtown streets, you'll notice many ornate buildings in "Victorian gingerbread" style. The upper levels of most of the town's buildings were destroyed during labour riots in 1878, and have been rebuilt in period style; the original Danish stone bases remain.

The mid-18th-century **outdoor market** is open some mornings, but an even better show is the picturesque seaside **fish market**, where all manner of exotic fish and seafood are bought and sold.

Around the Island

Just outside Frederiksted at La Grange, you can take a tour of the charming **Estate La Grange** and **Lawaetz Family Farm**, where a member of the Lawaetz family will conduct you on a tour of their gardens and eighteenth century home, filled with period antiques. A pleasant little coastal road runs north, meandering through the dense foliage of St Croix's small rainforest and on to the Virgin Islands' celebrated Carambola Golf Course.

Elsewhere on the north shore, marking the site where Columbus's crew came ashore on his second voyage, the **Salt River Bay National Historical Park** harbours a wide variety of endangered flora and fauna. Night-time kayak tours paddle through the bioluminescent waters of its main bay. in addition to a visitor centre.

A main highway, Centerline Road, crosses the island, to link its two towns. Near the western end is St Croix's proudest land-bound attraction, the **Estate Whim Museum**. You'll want to spend at least an hour on this elegant estate, with a Great House built by an eccentric Danish planter in 1794 and furnished with period antiques. A fascinating 1832 apothecary shop has been recreated, and the huge stone windmill and mule mill, both used to grind sugar, have been fully restored.

Farther east is **St George Village Botanical Garden**, set around the ruins of another Afro-Danish sugar cane plantation. South of Whim, the **Cruzan Rum Distillery**, still in working operation, offers a tour of the charming factory buildings. You will have a chance to sample the products at the end of the visit.

Christiansted

A small wedge of Christiansted, beginning at King's Wharf, was the heart of the Danish capital. It's preserved as the **Christiansted National Heritage Site** by the US National Park Service.

Overlooking the harbour , **Fort Christiansvaern** offers spectacular views over Gallows Bay. Built with bricks used as ballast on Danish ships, it's a formidable structure, though it was never fired on and the guns on the parapet were never used. Dating back to 1734, the neat yellow fort is the oldest structure on the island, though greatly restored.

Leaving the fort through the sally port, you any spy the **Steeple Building**, the island's first Danish Lutheran church.

Nearby stands the charming yellow-painted **Old Danish Customs House**, fronted with a sweeping staircase. Originally built in 1734, its second storey was added in 1830.

Government House on King Street has a narrow ballroom where the Danish elite drank and danced away the long colonial evenings. Not only governors but wealthy planter-merchants lived at times in this admired residence, part of which stood as early as 1747. The red wooden sentry box dates back to the Danish period.

Buck Island Reef National Monument

Any morning at the Christiansted wharf, take your choice of sloop, schooner, catamaran or glass-bottomed boat for the 9-km (5.5-mile) trip to this island off St Croix's northeastern shore. With its fabulous underwater trail through an encircling coral reef, the island was proclaimed a US National Monument by President John F. Kennedy in 1961. Boat skippers provide masks and fins, and there are various raft-glass viewing devices so that no one need miss the multitude of brightly coloured fish. You'll be guided along the natural trail, which has sunken arrows and signs identifying coral species which are perfectly visible in water no more than 4 m deep.

THE HARD FACTS

Airports. Lettsome (EIS) on Beef Island is 14 km (9 miles) from Road Town on Tortola. Virgin Gorda (VIJ) is 3 km (2 miles) from Spanish Town. Anegada (NGE) also has an airport. St Thomas (STT) is 3 km (2 miles) from Charlotte Amalie, and St Croix (STX) 18 km (10 miles) from Christiansted.

Climate. The Virgin Islands boast of the best weather in the Caribbean: cooling trade winds, lower humidity than elsewhere and an average annual temperature of 77°F (25°C). Rare is the day without predominantly blue sky and sunshine. Hurricane season is June to November.

Clothing. Dress is generally informal, but beachwear should be kept only for the beach. Take lightweight clothing.

Communications. The international country code for BVI is 1 284 49 and for USVI 1 340. The international dialling code from BVI is 00, from USVI 001. The major hotels provide Internet access, often wireless, and you will also find Internet cafés in the towns. Cruise-ship terminals and cafés/restaurants in all the Virgins' capitals and resorts offer wi-fi.

Customs Allowance. *BVI:* free import by passengers of 18 years and over of 200 cigarettes or 50 cigars or 225 g tobacco; 1 quart of wine or spirits. *USVI:* visitors over 21 may import duty-free 200 cigarettes or 100 cigars or 2 kg of tobacco; 1 quart spirits; otherwise duty must be paid on all imported gifts.

Driving. Driving is on the left. The maximum speed limit on BVI is 64 kph (40 mph); on USVI 35 kph (20 mph) in towns and 55 kph (35 mph) elsewhere. National licences are accepted in USVI but to hire a car on BVI you will need a temporary BVI licence, issued on production of a current foreign licence.

Electricity. BVI: 110 volts AC, 60 Hz, with sockets for 2-pin (flat) plugs. USVI: 120 volts AC, 60 Hz.

Emergencies. In the BVI, call 999 for police and fire service, 911 for an ambulance. In the USVI, call 911 for all emergency services.

Holidays. *All islands*: January 1, New Year's Day; March–April, Good Friday, Easter Monday; December 25–26, Christmas.

    BVI: March, Lavity Stoutt's Birthday, Commonwealth Day; June, Whit Monday, 2nd Saturday, Queen's Birthday; July 1, Territory Day; 1st Monday, Tuesday and Wednesday in August, festival days; October 21, St Ursula's Day.

    USVI: January 6, Three Kings' Day, 3rd Monday in January, Martin Luther King Day; February, Presidents' Day; March–April, Holy Thursday; May, Memorial Day; June, Organic Act Day; July 3 Danish West Indies Emancipation Day; July 4, US Independence Day; July, Hurricane Supplication Day; September, Labor Day; October, Columbus Day, Puerto Rico Friendship Day, Virgin Islands Thanksgiving Day; November 1, D. Hamilton Jackson Day; November, Veterans' Day, US Thanksgiving Day.

Language. English. Spanish and Creole are widely spoken in the US Virgin Islands.

Money. The official currency is the US dollar. The main credit cards are widely accepted.

Tipping. Taxi drivers expect a 15 percent tip. Major restaurants and nightclubs add a service charge to the bill; if not you can add 15 to 20 percent.

Tourist Information. For online information on the BVI, visit www.bvitourism.com; for the USVI, go to www.visitusvi.com.

Transport. Taxis cover standard journeys at fixed rates. They can also be hired on an hourly or daily basis. The drivers are excellent guides. A public bus service operates on St Thomas from Charlotte Amalie to Red Hook and Bordeaux.

Water. Town supplies are drinkable; bottled mineral water is available.

Benelux Press

Saba, Statia (Sint-Eustatius) and Sint Maarten

Near the top of the Eastern Caribbean islands—known collectively, alongside Bonaire, as the BES Islands—Saba and Statia are largely ignored by the tourism business, their sunny charm lying in their simplicity. While Saba is mountainous and rugged, Statia is green and lush. They have different flags, different capitals and three currencies, all in just 88 sq km (34 sq miles). Yet they share their idyllic, carefree lifestyle.

Sint Maarten (Saint-Martin in French) attracts more tourists, drawing shoppers to its Dutch side and food connoisseurs to its French side.

Dots in the Ocean

Saba, the tip of an extinct volcano, 45 km (28 miles) south of Sint Maarten, is the smallest of all the Dutch islands, covering a mere 13 sq km (5 sq miles). Next in size at 21 sq km (8 sq miles) comes Statia, 27 km (17 miles) to the southeast of Saba. Though both of the islands are special Dutch municipalities, most of the place names and conversations are nonetheless in English.

istockphoto.com/Li

Nestling in a valley, The Bottom is Saba's red-roofed capital. | Saba is formed from an extinct volcano and is a top scuba-diving destination.

The islands saw their heyday during the 18th century, when their riches were fought over by Spanish, French, English and Dutch. By Caribbean standards, Saba (1,800 inhabitants) and Statia (3,500) are poor islands, the traditional activities of agriculture, fishing and trading now supplemented by low-key tourism.

Either island can easily be seen in a day, but many devotees come for longer, to enjoy the peace and quiet and scenery, ranging from rugged rock to tropical gardens ablaze with flowers, and from meadows and farmland to steamy rainforest where man-sized ferns shade the mountain paths.

Saba

Its four villages—The Bottom, Windwardside, St John's and Hell's Gate—are strung out across the island, linked by a single road. Until the 1940s they could be reached only by steps hewn from the rock. When Dutch engineers were summoned to examine the possibility of building a road in the 1930s, they said it was impossible. Proving them wrong, a resourceful islander took a correspondence course in engineering and spent the next 20 years building a concrete thoroughfare that traverses the island's hilly interior, splitting in two at one point to avoid a tree.

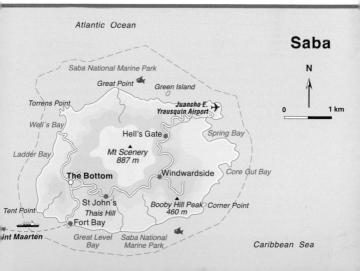

Saba

Atlantic Ocean

Saba National Marine Park
Great Point
Green Island
Torrens Point
Juancho E. Yrausquin Airport
Well's Bay
Hell's Gate
Spring Bay
Ladder Bay
Mt Scenery 887 m
The Bottom
Windwardside
Core Gut Bay
St John's
Thais Hill
Booby Hill Peak 460 m
Corner Point
Tent Point
Fort Bay
int Maarten
Great Level Bay
Saba National Marine Park
Caribbean Sea

N

0   1 km

SABA, STATIA & SINT MAARTEN FLASHBACK

16th–17th centuries
Columbus sights and names Sint Maarten in 1493; Saba is first sighted by Sir Francis Drake in 1595 and by Dutchman Pieter Schouten in 1624. In 1632 shipwrecked Englishmen land on uninhabited Saba, three years before France claims the island. The Dutch capture Sint Maarten in 1633, settle on Statia in 1636 and build Fort Oranje, then occupy Saba in the 1640s. The English, Dutch, French and Spanish dispute the islands.

18th century
Trade in sugar, tobacco and cotton brings slaves and prosperity to the islands, particularly Statia, which is nicknamed "The Golden Rock". During the American War of Independence, Statia is an important trans-shipment centre for guns and other supplies to American troops. In 1781, Admiral Rodney and his British soldiers ransack Fort Oranje. The following year the French arrive. During the first half of the 18th century, the British manage three short seizures of St Martin. The treaty ending the Seven Years' War (1756–1763) between Britain and France leaves French St Martin in Gallic hands. Sint Maarten remains Dutch.

19th century
In 1816 both Saba and Statia finally become Dutch, Saba having changed hands 12 times and Statia 22 in the preceding two and a half centuries. Ownership of St Martin is eventually shared between the Netherlands and France in the same year. The emancipation of plantation-working slaves on all the islands in the second half of the 19th century creates a labour shortage and hastens the decline of the islands, which sink to an existence dependent on subsistence from the sea and a few poor crops.

20th century–present
The French part of the St Martin is made a sub-prefecture of Guadeloupe in the 1940s. A charter in 1954 gives domestic autonomy to Saba and Statia but proclaims the islands an integral part of the Kingdom of the Netherlands. In July 2007, Saint-Martin separates from Guadeloupe and becomes an autonomous overseas territory. Following the break-up of the Netherlands Antilles, Saba, Statia and Sint Maarten are declared "special municipalities" of the Netherlands in 2010.

There are no beaches on Saba, apart from a single stretch of dark volcanic sand at **Well's Bay**.

The Bottom

Saba's minuscule capital is named for its location in a valley surrounded by hills, *botte* being the old Zeeland word for a bowl. Among the few sights are the **Sacred Heart Church**, with its pretty stained-glass windows, and the **Saba Artisan Foundation**, which produces some lovely souvenirs. Take a look, too, at **The Ladder** — 524 steps cut into the rock — once the sole means of access for passengers and cargo arriving by sea. On the way, stop by the **Major Osmar Ralph Simmons Museum**, a tiny display of domestic artefacts collected by a former police officer.

Windwardside

Saba's second largest settlement, almost 1,000 ft higher up, is an idyllic little village with red-roofed clapboard or white-washed houses and gardens full of colourful hibiscus and oleander.

The **Harry L. Johnson Museum** is housed in a sea captain's cottage around 150 years old, displaying interesting old family heirlooms, including a mahogany four-poster bed. At **Jo Bean's Hot Glass Studio**, you can watch glass beads being made and even have a go yourself.

Peaks

On the outskirts of Windwardside, 1,064 hand-hewn steps lead to the top of 887 m **Mount Scenery**, Saba's highest point, often with its head in the clouds. Much less strenuous are the 60 steps up to the 460 m **Bobby Hill Peak**, which its offers more panoramic views as well as hiking trails.

Saba Marine Park

With good visibility down to a depth of 30 m or more, an increasing number of snorkellers and divers are being lured to this underwater wonderland of caverns and corals, home to a multitude of fish and sealife. In an effort to preserve Saba's marvellous heritage, the extensive Saba Marine Park was established in 1987. The park office at Fort Bay can give information about lessons, equipment hire and trips.

Statia

"Statia" is a contraction of "St Anastasia", the original name bestowed on the island by Columbus. The Dutch preferred Sint Eustatius but the original abbreviation stuck.

Oranjestad

Pick up a walking tour brochure from the tourist office and enjoy a stroll through the quaint streets of the capital, more a village than a city, filled with small, Dutch-style houses. The chief monument is the extensively restored **Fort Oranje**, put up in 1636 in an attempt to guard against intruders, and added to by the British in 1703. Complete with cannon and a parade ground, the fort is a great lookout spot and provides a glimpse into the island's history.

For more insight into the past, visit the 18th-century Doncker-de Graaff House, now home to the **Sint Eustatius Historical Foundation Museum**. The island's prosperous heyday is brought alive in its exhibits and reconstructed rooms, and there's also a section illustrating pre-Hispanic history, including the 1,500-year-old skeleton of an Arawak Indian.

Other sights worth a peek are the warehouses and taverns, some undergoing restoration, and the 18th-century places of worship with their adjoining graveyards—**Honen Dalim Synagogue**, built in 1738, and the **Dutch Reformed Church**—all attesting to the rise and fall of the island's fortunes.

Hikes

The interior is sparsely populated, and large areas are untouched by human hand. If you're a nature lover, you'll find interesting hiking through the tropical forests. The tourist office can provide details of the various trails, for some of which you may need a guide.

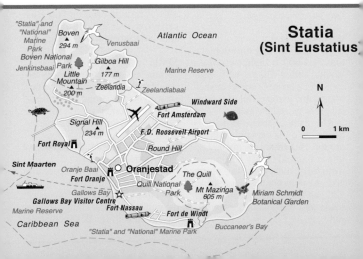

DINING AND SHOPPING

On the menu

Sopito makes a good starter. This tasty fish and coconut soup is flavoured with salt pork and assorted spices. Hearty island hors-d'œuvres include *funchi* (maize or cornmeal patties), *ayacas* (plantain or banana leaves stuffed with a maize meal and meat filling), and *calas* (mashed beans fried in batter).

For the main courses: *keshi yena*, Edam cheese stuffed with meat, chicken or fish and raisins, then baked, and *capucijners*, a combination of beans, bacon, onions and pickles. *Stoba*, the famous Caribbean goast stew (sometimes made with lamb), is also very popular on these islands.

Don't miss the chance to sample authentic Indonesian *rijsttafel*, an array of 20 to 30 different and flavourful dishes served with rice. You will get wildly hot *sambal* on the side—lime juice and chilli peppers with a paste of roasted shrimp or fish.

In addition to a wide choice of non-alcoholic drinks, all the famous Dutch beers are available, including Amstel and Heineken.

The best buys

From Saba, bring home a bottle or two of Saba Spice as a souvenir. By far the best buy in Saba is the fine linen featuring the intricate drawn-thread needlework known as Saba lace, or Spanish work, introduced from South America more than a century ago. Examples of this fine craftwork include handkerchiefs and napkins.

Statia is known for traditional woodwork and silk-screen printing on cotton. Island scenes in watercolours will be a permanent reminder of your visit to these shores.

istockphoto.com/...ucaci

A popular goal is the rather steep climb to **The Quill**, the extinct volcano that dominates the island's silhouette, protected as part of the **Quill/Boven National Park**. Its rainforest crater is full of breadfruit trees, orchids and lianas, as well as land crabs that the locals catch to put in the pot. The **Gallows Bay Visitor Centre** offers guided hikes and information.

Adjacent to the park, the **Miriam Schmidt Botanical Garden** has sections devoted to palms, herbs and the senses, as well as a lookout spot and a birdwatching trail.

Beaches

Statia's beaches don't live up to most people's idea of an idyllic palm-fringed stretch of sand. **Oranje Beach**, near the capital, is safe for swimming and watersports. The beaches on the windward, Atlantic side are sandy and scenic, but are unsafe because of the strong undertow. Designated as the **Statia National Marine Park**, the waters round the island provide excellent diving and snorkelling, with several wrecks to explore. The Gallows Bay Visitor Centre has information on scuba operators and equipment hire.

Playing pan in Sint Maarten. | The Saban anole (Anolis sabanus) is endemic to the island. | A great eagle ray sports magnificent patterns.

istockphoto.com/CaptLensCap

istockphoto.com/Valtenbergs

wikimedia.org/Bosset

Sint Maarten

The island can qualify as having one of the world's longest governmental love affairs: since 1648 the French and Dutch have shared sovereignty in almost total harmony, and the frontier between the two remains unguarded. The island is free of levies on any imports, which means duty-free shopping with goods half the price of those in Europe.

Philipsburg

A popular stopover for cruise ships, the Dutch capital is a lively place, its wooden churches, painted houses and Indonesian restaurants vying for space with luxury hotels. It also has the island's only international airport, gateway for most visitors and close to the best beaches.

Front Street (Voorstraat), parallel to the shore, is the main thoroughfare lined with hotels, casinos, restaurants and, of course, duty-free shops. Most of the sites are to be found on this street: the old **Courthouse**, with a little bell tower, dating from 1793; the pretty **Methodist Church** of 1851; and, at No. 7, the small **Sint Maarten Museum** tracing the history of the island. Outside the courthouse, near the waterfront, is the lively **Cyrus Wathey Square**. Run by a *Star Wars* special-effects artist, the **Yoda Guy Movie Exhibit** at 19A displays props from the movies.

Around Philipsburg

On the **Pointe Blanche**, on the eastern part of the **Great Bay**, **Bobby's Marina** is one of the major boat yards in the northeastern Caribbean. Boats depart for St Barthélémy (no passport needed) and other islands.

At the other end of the peninsula closing the bay in the west, **Fort Amsterdam** was the first fort to be built by Dutch settlers in the Caribbean, in 1631. It lies in ruins, but affords fabulous views over the bay and the core foundations of **Fort Willem I**. First built by the British in 1801 under the name of Fort Tigge, the latter was renamed by the Dutch as a tribute to the King of Holland.

Sint Maarten Park north of the Great Salt Pond (Madame Estate, Arch Road) has a botanical garden and a small zoo with over 80 species of animals including exotic parrots. West of the park are the ruins of the **Sucker Garden salt factory**, built in 1852.

Beaches

Beyond the airport are some of the best of the island's 37 beaches: **Simpson Bay**, **Mullet Bay** and **Maho Bay**, famous for the jumbo jets that fly right over it in their final descent to the airport. Sapphire blue or emerald green, the water is irresistible at them all. **Dawn Beach** in the northeast is the prettiest on the island.

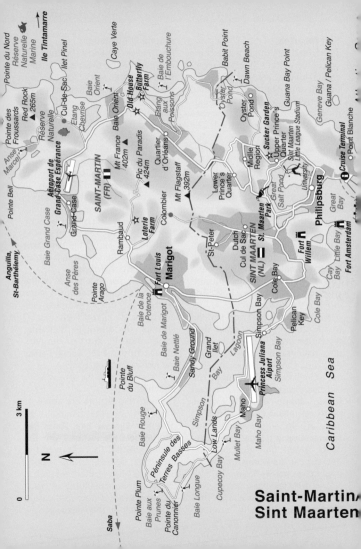

THE HARD FACTS

Communications. The area code for Saba, Satia and Sint-Maarten is 599. You can use your own mobile phone on all the islands, but roaming costs are high; local SIM cards are cheap and widely available. Sint Maarten's cruise terminal has an Internet café, and wi-fi is available at most hotels as well as at bars and restaurants in larger towns and resorts.

Climate. The islands have warm weather year-round, with average temperatures most often between 24° and 29° C (75° and 85° F).

Clothing. Dress is generally informal, but beachwear should be kept only for the beach. Take tropical, lightweight clothing.

Emergencies. Statia: police 911; fire service 912; ambulance 913. Sint Maarten: police 911, fire service 919, ambulance 910. Saba: Police, fire service and ambulance 911.

Language. The official language is Dutch, and many people also speak English, Spanish and Paplamento, a mixture of Dutch, French, English, Spanish, Portuguese and several African languages.

Money. The US dollar is the official currency of Saba and Statia. On Sint Maarten, offcial currency is the Netherlands Antilles guilder or florin (NAf or ANG), divided into 100 cents, but U.S. dollars, Euros and major credit cards are widely accepted.

Time. UTC/GMT−4, all year round.

Tipping. Taxi drivers expect a 15 percent tip. Major restaurants add a service charge to the bill, but inexpensive places do not normally do so: in such cases you can add 15 to 20 percent for good service.

Transport. Taxi rates are fixed, and larger islands have car rental companies and a public bus service.

Water. Bottled mineral water is available everywhere.

istockphoto.com/StockWorthy

MONTSERRAT

A mere dot in the northern Leeward chain, coverin 104 sq km (39 sq miles), Montserrat is just 11 km (7 miles) long and 16 km (10 miles) across at its widest point. Settled by Spanish and British, and from 1632 by Irish Catholics fleeing religious oppression on St Kitts, the island became a plantation colony with sugar as the main crop. After the abolition of slavery in 1834, sugar was replaced by limes and other orchard and market-garden crops. Together with Antigua, St Kitts, Nevis and Anguilla, Montserrat was incorporated in the Territory of the Leeward Islands in 1956 and joined the Federation Of the West Indies two years later. Independence was offered in 1966, but the island chose to remain a British Crown Colony. A modest tourist industry developed, but in 1989, disaster struck and Hurricane Hugo caused widespread damage. Then in 1995, the Soufrière Hills volcano began to erupt, reaching a climax in 1997, when it covered the island in a blanket of mud and ash. More than half the population fled to Britain and elsewhere, and Plymouth, the capital, was destroyed; it's now at Brades in the northwest. The volcano is still active and the southeastern half of the island is an exclusion zone, which you can tour with an authorised guide if volcanic activity has been low. Otherwise, you can view Plymouth from afar at Garibaldi Hill or Richmond, and visit the Montserrat Volcano Observatory (Monday to Thursday) in Flemings.

istockphoto.com/Hannah

Anguilla

Imagine a long, slender coral island lying lazily in the eastern Caribbean, with more than thirty superlative beaches fringing its shores. Then visualize the vibrant marine life in its coral reefs waiting to be explored. That's Anguilla. Best of all, you can still have some of those beaches virtually to yourself, despite the increasing numbers of visitors.

Terrific and Tranquil

The population of 17,000 is descended mostly from Africans, although the arrival of many North Americans and Europeans has created an interesting cultural mosaic. Traditionally the islanders have lived from salt production, lobster fishing, agriculture and livestock. It's a friendly, quiet place, and one of the safest in the Caribbean. Tourism is now the major source of revenue. Boat races are frequently held here; the craft are unique wooden sloops made locally. The most noteworthy races take place during Carnival Week in August, leaving from Sandy Ground beach and are enlivened by non-stop parties.

The low-lying coral island is covered with scrub vegetation. While there's no lack of nightlife, you may prefer to go to bed early and get up with the dawn to swim with the iridescent fish of the reef or sunbathe on the white sands.

The Valley

The capital, set in the centre of the island, has a population of 2,000. You can explore **Wallblake House**, a plantation house with period furnishings as well as a restored stable block and workers' quarters, but most visitors never stir from the beachy fringes of the island to investigate The Valley. Visit the **National Trust of Anguilla** office to book a heritage walking tour.

Beaches

Whichever one of the 33 magnificent beaches you decide on, you can arrange for a taxi to take you there and pick you up later. Here are the best, running anti-clockwise from Shoal Bay (East), on the northeast coast.

Shoal Bay (East)

This is the most popular beach, and it has more facilities than the others, including beach chairs, umbrellas, snorkels, masks and paddle boats for rent. Snorkelling is easy as pie here, with the closest reef only a stone's throw offshore. A glass-bottom boat makes trips over the reef, and you can hire a fishing boat.

The Fountain, discovered near Shoal Bay, is a cavern containing several freshwater pools, a spring and some petroglyphs. Archaeologists believe this dome-shaped cavern was a major Arawak centre for worship.

ANGUILLA FLASHBACK

Pre-Columbian era
The island is inhabited by Arawaks, until the warlike Carib tribe arrive and take over. In 1493 Columbus sights the island and names it Anguilla ("eel"), probably because of its long, thin shape.

17th century
The British colonize the island in 1650. Many of the settlers are Irish from St Kitts. The Amerindians are wiped out by enslavement and disease.

18th century
The population numbers over 1,000, two-thirds of whom are African slaves. The French attack in 1745 and 1796, but are repelled by the islanders.

19th century
Anguilla is incorporated into the colony of St Kitts and Nevis.

20th century–present
In 1967 Anguilla makes a unilateral declaration of independence and expels the St Kitts police force. As negotiations break down between the islanders and the Crown, British paratroopers "invade" the island in 1969 and install a Commissioner. The London Metropolitan Police maintain an unusual presence on the island until 1972. Anguilla becomes a British Dependent Territory in 1980, with a Governor to represent the Crown. Tourism becomes important.

St Gerard's Church in The Valley.

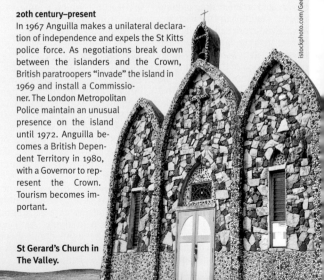

istockphoto.com/Geer

At the nearby fishing village, **Island Harbour**, you can explore the eclectic displays at the **Heritage Collection Museum,** ranging from Arawak finds to natural history. You can get transport to many of the cays and islands. **Scilly Cay**, out in the harbour, is one of these: you just have to wave from the shore and a boat will come out to collect you.

Little Bay

Protected by high cliff walls extending into the sea, this is a hideaway beach where you may see shoals of silver fish shimmering in the blue water. Swim around the cliff wall to the north and you will reach **Limestone Bay**, a tiny stretch of sand on the Atlantic coast.

Crocus Bay

At the bottom of a steep hill, Crocus Bay offers excellent snorkelling, views of cliffs and fantastic sunsets. If you are lucky you may see fishermen hauling in their trawl nets.

Sandy Ground/Road Bay

Sandy Ground sees a lot of action as the principal port on the island; it has a lively nightlife and plenty of restaurants. One of the busiest is the *Pumphouse*, a former salt factory which processed salt collected at the nearby Road Salt Pond, and still bedecked with memorabilia from its former life. Regular ferries make the short journey to **Sandy Island**, known for its excellent snorkelling.

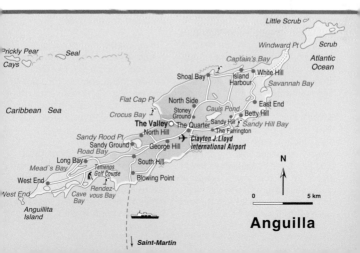

Anguilla

istockphoto.com/McFarlane

A phone link to home directly from the beach.

Further out are **Prickly Pear Cays** with a sweeping arc of sand, a large population of birds and pelicans, and superb coral gardens. Road Bay beach is quiet and ideal for swimming.

Mead's Bay
The mile-long beach has sands like talcum powder, calm blue waters and some fine restaurants and beach bars. **Malliouhana Resort** is at the eastern end, **Frangipani** and **Carimar Beach Club** to the west, but in between these resorts you can still find plenty of solitude.

Cove Bay
With dunes and coconut palms and just one restaurant, this is a secluded beach; its reef is popular with snorkellers.

Rendezvous Bay
A perfect arc of dune-lined sand, this is the longest of Anguilla's beaches and it offers great walking opportunities. Pretty shells wash up onto the soft white sand.

Blowing Point
A sea port with links to St-Martin, Blowing Point has small beaches on both sides. To the east is a small cove with a salt pond which is perfect for bird-watching.

Little Harbour
Hemmed in by low cliffs and an offshore reef, the beach here is secluded and shallow.

Sandy Hill Bay
A tiny, protected bay with a sloping, sandy beach that's perfect for children, and popular for family picnics. The snorkelling area offshore has small coral formations and green underwater meadows.

Windward Point Bay
Wild and windswept, at the island's northeast point and reached by bumpy road or a hike from Junk's Hole. Carry on to rugged, wave-shipped **Captain's Bay** on the north shore.

Antigua and Barbuda

This is not the place for those who want things done by yesterday. The pace of life is easy—Antigua and Barbuda's 90,000 people take their time. That is why cricket is popular—more than a national sport, it's almost a religion.

Corbis/Krist

The game of *warri* is popular in Antigua; the name means "house" and refers to the hollows carved into the wooden board.

Antigua

The outline is what gives Antigua its special attraction—scores of bays and inlets, set with so many beaches that you can stay there a year and never visit the same beach twice. There are 365 of them and they are reckoned to be among the finest in the world. The capital, St John's, is easy to explore on foot

St John's

Cruise ships anchor on **Heritage Quay**, adjacent to the city centre and packed with shops, cafes and restaurants. The attractive cut-stone buildings of Redcliffe Quay offer more of the same; for a touch of local flavour, head up to **Market Street** where the covered market is a riot of colour and smells, with piles of earthy yams, dasheen and tropical fruit.

St John's Cathedral is one of the most interesting Anglican churches in the Caribbean. Originally a wooden construction of 1683, it has been rebuilt twice. After the 1843 earthquake de-stroyed the previous cathedral, a structure designed to be quake- and hurricane-proof was devised of pitch pine encased in stone. The stone figures adorning the south gate are said to have been taken from one of Napoleon's ships.

The 18th-century Court House, the former seat of justice and parliament, now houses the **National Museum of Antigua and Barbuda**. It contains some fascinating displays on the history of the islands and sporting memorabilia.

To the northwest, overlooking the harbour, are the ruins of **Fort James** (1706), which once guarded St John's in pirate days. Vestiges of the ramparts still stand and its cannons point out to sea.

English Harbour

One of the most fascinating historical sites of the Caribbean is **Nelson's Dockyard** at English Har-

ANTIGUA AND BARBUDA
FLASHBACK

15th–16th centuries
Columbus sights the island, inhabited by Arawak Indians, on his second voyage in 1493 and names it after the church of Santa María la Antigua in Seville.

17th century
English planters from St Kitts colonize Antigua in 1632. The island is coveted by the French and Spanish, but apart from a brief and bloodless French occupation in 1666, it remains British until independence. Antigua becomes the seat of government of the "Leeward Caribbee Islands". In 1680 the British lease Barbuda to the English Codrington brothers, Christopher and John, who had established the island's first sugar plantation 11 years earlier. However, the plantation system is not compatible with Barbuda's infertile soil and poor rainfall. The Codringtons use Barbuda instead to grow supplies and raise animals for their Antigua sugar estates. They also bring in African slaves to work the plantations.

18th century
American independence robs Antigua and other islands of their markets, and the plantation economy declines. English Harbour becomes the main British naval base in the Caribbean. Rodney sets out from here to defeat the French fleet in 1782 and to regain Britain's West Indies possessions. Nelson is stationed here in the 1780s as commander-in-chief of the Leeward Islands squadron.

19th century
After the Napoleonic Wars the island's strategic importance declines. An earthquake in 1843 hastens the ruin of the sugar plantations. In 1860 Barbuda is made a dependency of Antigua, which becomes part of a federated Leeward Islands Colony in 1871 and retains the seat of government.

20th century–present
Antigua and Barbuda becomes one of the West Indies Associated States of Britain in 1967 with a new constitution and self-government. Agriculture is revived. Independence is attained in 1981. Louise Lake-Tack becomes the first female governor-general in July 2007.

bour. Developed in the mid-18th century to shelter British warships protecting the West Indies possessions, it saw its heyday during the War of American Independence and the wars against the French. Admiral Horatio Nelson made it his base in the 1780s, but when ships became too big to negotiate the near-landlocked harbour, the dockyard went into decline and was abandoned in 1889. With growing awareness of the island's tourist potential, it was restored during the 1950s, and is now a burgeoning tourist centre. The Admiral's House is furnished in period style and now houses the **Dockyard Museum**, while other cut-stone buildings house restaurants and bars.

Dow's Hill Interpretation Centre

A short sound-and-light show illustrates six eras of Antigua's history. The centre also offers fine views over English and Falmouth harbours and **Galleon Beach**.

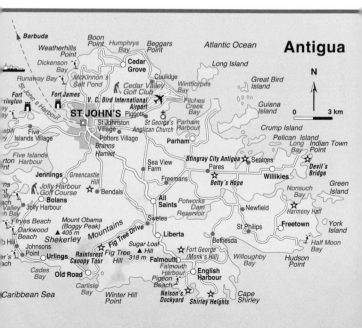

DINING AND SHOPPING

On the menu

On Antigua, black pudding is an adapted European dish and the familiar blood sausage has a highly spiced variant here. Favourite island dishes are pepperpot, a spicy meat and vegetable stew; *souse*, which is boiled pig's head and trotters served with lime juice, sliced cucumber and pepper; and *coo-coo*, cornmeal cooked with okra and the national dish of Antigua and Barbuda, where it's called *fungee*. *Doucanah* is a sweet potato dumpling flavoured with coconut and raisins, traditionally boiled in banana leaves. It is served with saltfish, anchovies and eggplant. In Dominica, you'll hear about "mountain chicken", actually a giant land frog, but now too endangered to be offered up on any menus; while in Montserrat, "goat water" is a fortifying soup of goat simmered together with yams, breadfruit and pumpkin. Barbados is known for its flying fish, served up with coo-coo. In St Vincent and the Grenadines, look out for the delicious national dish of fried, seasoned jackfish served with roasted breadfruit, the latter a delicious starchy fruit originally brought to the Caribbean by Captain Bligh on the famous *HMS Bounty*.

The best buys

An unusual souvenir from Antigua or Barbuda is a warri board—the equivalent of backgammon. You will also see red clay pottery and clay charcoal pots for grilling fish and meat. At The Valley post office in Anguilla, you'll find attractive stamps. Barbados rum is said by some to be the region's best, from light white rums that make great cocktails to aged dark rums that should be sipped and savoured. The Dominicans make pretty straw mats called *khus-khus* with geometric patterns, flower or fish motifs. On St Vincent and the Grenadines look for Sea Island cotton clothes; mahogany carvings; postage stamps; palm-frond sunhats woven right there on the beach.

Shirley Heights

Past Dow's Hill, and named for the English governor who built the fortifications here in 1787, Shirley Heights is set on a hilltop and provides fantastic views down over English Harbour. The restaurant has a steel band and barbecue on Sunday nights.

Fig Tree Drive

The scenic route back to St John's takes you through banana groves, hills and forest. Stop and buy a black pineapple at one of the fruit stalls, or some local art at the **Fig Tree Gallery**. At the **Antigua Rainforest Zip Line Tour**, you can swing along 12 ziplines or try an adventurous treetop ropewalk.

Betty's Hope

In the centre of the island, this restored cut-stone sugar mill is a vestige of Antigua's once-thriving sugar industry.

Stingray City Antigua

Take a swim and hand-feed gentle, friendly rays at this enjoyable attraction just off the northeast coast near Seatons.

Beaches

The island's main resort is northwest of St John's, around **Dickenson Bay**. There are many other hotel complexes along the west coast, such as **Galley Bay**, **Hawksbill Bay**, **Turner's**, **Ffreyes** and **Darkwood**.

The most beautiful beach, with immaculate white sands and crystalline turquoise waters, is that of **Valley Church Bay**. In the southeast of the island, the wild **Half Moon Bay** is well worth a detour.

Barbuda

From St John's airport, it's a 15-minute flight to the sister island of Barbuda, 160 sq km (62 sq miles) of low scrub fringed by a magnificent beach around a lagoon. Most of its 1,500 inhabitants live in the island's only village, **Codrington**. Barbuda's association with Antigua goes back to the 17th century, when it was the private fiefdom of the Codrington family, who used it to raise provisions for their sugar plantations on Antigua and to run a sordid "breeding" colony for slaves.

Barbudans look upon their land as communally owned, and local custom dictates that property can only be leased and not sold to non-Barbudans, and then only by unanimous consent of all the inhabitants. This has allowed the island to remain pretty much devoid of major resort infrastructure. Visitors can enjoy undeveloped pink-sand beaches, go deep-sea fishing, snorkelling and scuba-diving round the reefs where there are more than 70 wrecks to explore. **Codrington Lagoon** supports one of the world's largest frigate bird colonies.

French Antilles

Guadeloupe, the largest of the French Islands, spreads its wings midway along the Lesser Antilles chain. Its administrative dependencies are Les Saintes, Marie-Galante and Désirade. Saint-Martin and Saint-Barthélemy are now French Overseas Collectivities. Martinique Island is 160 km (100 miles) further south.

Rooftops overlooking Orient Bay on Saint-Martin provide a spash of colour.

Saint-Martin

Much of the French side's charm is that it seems content to slumber languidly in the sun. Lingering over a seaside dinner is the preferred after-dark activity. You can also choose to take an island tour and visit the previously described Dutch side of the island.

Marigot

Marigot, the main town and capital of Saint-Marin, lies north of the Simpson Bay Lagoon.

The big marina of **Port La Royale** and luxury boutiques make this the main shopping area on the French side. Near the quayside, the morning market brings a touch of colour to the port. The archaeological museum, **Sur les Traces des Arawaks**, explores the island's pre-Columbian history. From there, it is a short climb to the deserted **Fort St-Louis**. This 18th-century bastion gives you a marvellous view over Marigot Bay.

Around the Island

A narrow road climbs to the 424 m summit of the **Pic du Paradis**, which offers fine views. At its foot is **Loterie Farm**, where you can visit one of the last stretches of tropical forest on the island, zipline through the canopy or swim in a spring-fed pool.

At the east-coast **Butterfly Farm**, south of Orient Bay, hundreds of beautifully hued butterflies flit through an enclosed garden.

Beaches

On the east coast, **Anse Marcel** is rather quiet; **Orient Beach**, a marvellous stretch of white sand lapped by crystal-clear waters is one of the best. Trips from here take you to **Ilet Pinel** and **Caye Vert**, small islets close to shore, or, further out to sea, **Tintamarre Island**. In the west, on the Terres Basses peninsula, consider **Baie Rouge**, **Baie aux Prunes** and **Baie Longue**.

FRENCH ANTILLES FLASHBACK

Pre-Columbian era

Indians from the Orinoco basin in South America migrate up the Antilles chain, reaching Martinique and Guadeloupe by AD 200. They are followed by the Arawaks (Igneri), another wave of Amerindians from the Orinoco in present-day Venezuela, who settle throughout the Caribbean by AD 300. Their tranquillity is shattered by the arrival of the Caribs.

15th–17th centuries

Christopher Columbus discovers Guadeloupe and Saint-Martin in 1493 and Martinique in 1502. The French start colonizing Martinique in 1635, but it takes them several years to prevail against the Caribs. Sugar plantations thrive in the 1640s and slaves are brought from Africa to work the fields. The French stake a claim in St-Barthélemy in 1648 and send Huguenot settlers from Brittany and Normandy in 1674.

18th–19th centuries

Britain and France battle for domination of the Antilles. Britain conquers Guadeloupe in 1759 and holds it for four years, and occupies Martinique for eight years from 1794. In 1784 Louis XVI gives St Barthélemy to Sweden in exchange for duty-free trading rights in Gothenburg. In 1848, the philanthropist Victor Schoelcher, Martinique's greatest hero, succeeds in having a law passed in France abolishing slavery. Ten years later, the law is implemented, freeing 87,500 slaves in Guadeloupe and 72,000 in Martinique. Contract workers begin to arrive from India and Africa to replace slave labour on the plantations. France buys back St Barthélemy from Sweden in 1878 for 320,000 gold francs.

20th century–present

Mont Pelée in Martinique erupts devastatingly in 1902, leaving more than 30,000 dead. In 1939, St. Martin receives a major boost to its post-slavery agricultural slump when it is declared a duty-free port. Its airport is remodelled in 1964, heralding the start of a growing tourist industry. Guadeloupe and Martinique become *départements* of France in 1946. Later, under an administrative reshuffle, they are renamed *régions*, each with a *préfet* named in Paris. In 2003 Guadeloupe acquires the status of a Région d'Outre-mer (ROM) and a Départment (DOM). In 2012 St-Barthélemy withdraws from the EU but still uses the Euro.

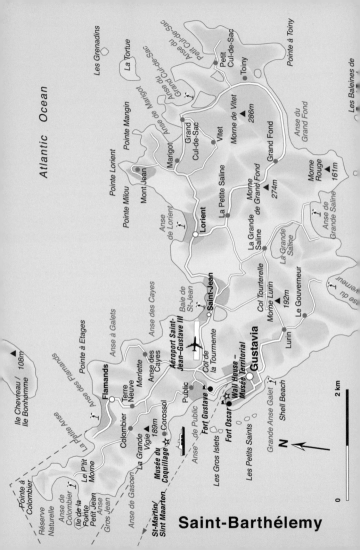

Saint-Barthélemy

This just might be the best piece of France anywhere. Known as "St Barts" or St-Barth in French (Columbus gave his brother's name, Bartholomew, to the island when he sailed past in 1493), it is peaceful and picturesque, with arid rollercoaster hills, hidden rocky coves and powdery beaches lining a limpid, emerald sea.

St Barts is a world apart. Many of the 9,000 inhabitants are descendants of Huguenots from Brittany and Normandy who arrived in the 17th century. The land was not very fertile, but the settlers' perseverance paid off: the island has become synonymous with luxury tourism since it was discovered by American millionaires, in the wake of Rockefeller. At many places off St Barts and around its rocky islets, there is fine reef snorkelling.

Gustavia

You'll soon understand why Gustavia's rectangular harbour is a favourite with the Caribbean yachting set. The Swedes declared it a free port in 1785, a status it still enjoys.

The best place to see it all is from the ruins of the old **Fort Gustav**, looking out over the red rooftops of the houses scattered among the hills; the opposite **Fort Oscar** is occupied by the gendarmerie. Down at the harbour you can rent small excursion- or fishing boats, or charter a floating palace. Or join the onlooking landlubbers at one of the cafés ringing the harbour.

Here and there you'll note a Swedish touch: the Swedish flag beside the French on St Barts' coat of arms; the old Swedish clocktower in green-painted wood; the shopping streets bearing Swedish names and the old Dinzey house, now the Swedish consulate.

Look into the venerable **Wall House Museum** (Musée Territorial) with a wide-ranging set of historical displays, and visit the Anglican and Catholic churches.

The West

The seascapes and panoramas on this island are enough to tempt any driver to glance away from the serviceable but narrow roads. Winding and hilly, they are veritable labyrinths, many finishing at signposted dead-ends. From Gustavia, a road leads to the **Col de la Tourmente**, a crossroads where the main activity is watching the planes skimming over the hilltop before diving into the airport at St-Jean Bay. Branch roads take you to northwards to the beautiful **Anse des Cayes**, to **Flamands**, a pretty village set along a curving beach (the current can be strong here), and finally to **Petite Anse**.

Coconut palms and sloping cliffs ring the tranquil waters of **Colombier**, with the superb tan sands of **Anse de Colombier** beach, reachable only by boat or a 20-minute walk. You can see the hazy outline of St-Martin out to sea. Returning to Gustavia via the west coast, you will come to **Corossol**, where the fascinating **Musée de Coquillages** displays over 9,000 seashells from local beaches, collected by a local man since his childhood.

Kiss-me-not. For Sunday mass, old ladies in St-Barthélemy used to wear the white cotton bonnets brought here by their Norman ancestors three centuries ago. Their French name, *quichenotte*, may derive from the English kiss-me-not; it probably protected delicate cheeks from the hot sun, though it's said it was invented to stop English soldiers dallying with French women.

hemis.fr/Du Boisberranger

The East

There is no access problem to **St-Jean**, the best known of St Barthélemy's beaches, with excellent swimming in two shimmering crescents of pale sand separated by a small rocky promontory and sheltered by a coral reef.

Further east, **Lorient** was the island's first settlement. Visit the church built with local stone, hauled here by boat and filed down to size by the townswomen. Inside, conch shells do duty as holy water basins.

Not far away is **Pointe Milou**, a wild headland from which, on a clear day, you can count nine isles or rocks in the sea. The strange cactus-like plants with red nobbles are named *Têtes à l'Anglais* (Englishman's heads) after the British redcoats.

From the highest point of the road encircling **Morne Vitet**, on the eastern part of the island, stop to take in the sweeping view over a bay called **Grand Cul-de-Sac**, favoured by windsurfers, and out to Tortue islet in the Atlantic. The bay of **Petit Cul-de-Sac** is backed by a pool that serves as a stopover for migratory birds.

The wilder south coast has two pleasant beaches in neighbouring coves: **Grande Saline** and **Gouverneur**. Sea grapes and shrubs provide little shade here; otherwise you should find no fault with either of these strands.

Guadeloupe

The island we know as Guadeloupe is in fact made up of two separate isles linked by a drawbridge across a salt-water channel, the Rivière Salée (Salt River). On a map, it resembles a butterfly. The component islands are notably dissimilar. Grande-Terre is the smaller, drier and flatter of the two. It is the site of Pointe-à-Pitre, the commercial centre and largest city. The administrative capital, Basse-Terre, is located on the other island, also called Basse-Terre — literally, Low Land — nestling at the foot of the famous Soufrière volcano.

Pointe-à-Pitre

A tiny fishing village three centuries ago, this city is named after a Dutchman, Pieter, said to have been the most popular fishmonger on the waterfront. Don't miss the fruit and vegetable market near the wharves, where fishing boats lie at anchor in the mornings. There's also a craft market on Quai Gatine, opposite.

Place de la Victoire

Facing the harbour, the café-lined square sprawls in the shade of royal palms. The Victory of its name recalls the defeat of the English in 1795 — when the governor Victor Hugues set up a guillotine here that made short work of more than 4,000 white settlers.

Just off the square, the **Basilique St-Pierre et St-Paul** (1807) features unusual metal columns and balconies. It has been destroyed three times by hurricanes, each time restored to its former glory. Nearby, the **tourist office** is on Quai Perrinon.

Town Centre

Pointe-à-Pitre bustles by day and empties at night. Along Rue Frébault, the shops spill out over the pavement. On the corner of Rue Peynier, the **central market** is the place to buy local spices and rum-based drinks.

In a restored colonial mansion on Rue de Nozières, **Musée St-John Perse** is devoted to this venerable poet, born Alexis Leger in Pointe-à-Pitre, who won the 1960 Nobel Prize for Literature. In Rue Peynier, the **Musée Schoelcher** recounts the abolition of slavery and displays Schoelcher's art collection.

There's another moving commemoration to the slave strade just south in Darboussier, where **Mémorial ACTe** occupies a stunning metal-shrouded building on the waterfront that opened in 2015.

Southern Grande-Terre

The beach-studded coast from Bas du Fort to St-François is Guadeloupe's main resort area, while the east coast is pounded by the wild Atlantic waves.

Bas du Fort

Three formidable cannon greet you at the wooden drawbridge entrance to the ruins of coral-stone **Fleur d'Epée** fort, presiding over Pointe-à-Pitre's harbour. Late in the 18th century, British and French forces fought bloody battles for this strategic hill, which offers panoramic views.

In a residential and touristic area below the fort, near the marina, the **Aquarium de la Guadeloupe** has pools with sharks, turtles, piranhas and local fish.

Le Gosier

Contingents of fierce invaders once put ashore here, but today, this is the start of Guadeloupe's riviera, with resort hotels strung along the beaches. From the village you look out over the turquoise bay and its superb protected islet.

Sainte-Anne

The island's best beach is near the former sugar capital Sainte-Anne: **La Caravelle**, owned by Club Med but open to the public. The coral reefs are clearly visible beneath the limpid water.

St-François

This old fishing village has been completely engulfed by hotels and resort facilities: glitzy marina, golf course, tennis courts, beaches. You can practise almost every sport imaginable here, and gamble in the casino. Just to the west of town, **Raisins Clairs** is a magnificent golden-sand beach.

La Pointe des Châteaux

At the eastern tip of Guadeloupe's butterfly wing, and protected as an ONF Reserve, this is a wildly beautiful region of limestone cliffs, eroded into castle-like shapes by Atlantic waves. The views of this rugged section of coastline are magnificent: the large island in the distance is La Désirade. Superb beaches here include **Plage des Salines**, the nudist **Anse Tarare**, and **Anse à la Gourde**.

Le Moule

From St-François, the road to Le Moule runs through great fields of sugar-cane dotted here and there with ruined sugar mills *(sucrotes)*, reminders of plantation days. Tours of the **Distillerie Damoiseau** at Bellevue give some insight into the rum-making process—and, of course, tastings are available.

The once-flourishing port of Le Moule has a charming beach, **L'Autre Bord**, bordered by almond and coconut trees, and the **Musée archéologique Edgar Clerc**, housing an interesting collection of pre-Columbian artefacts dating from Arawak and Carib times.

SUGAR CANE

The origins of the cultivation of sugar cane *(Saccharum officinarum)* are lost in the mists of time. However, it is believed that it was used for the first time in the Ganges basin. The word "sugar", derived from the Sanskrit "sarkara", tends to prove this theory. Brought to the Mediterranean by Arab merchants, sugar was unknown in Europe until after the Crusades, and at first it was called "pagan honey". For several centuries it was a luxury product, reserved for the elite. On his second journey, Christopher Columbus introduced sugar cane to America. Cultivation developed in the English and French islands from the second half of the 17th century, and soon afterwards, rum was invented. In the early days, sugar was exported to Europe in the form of syrup or molasses, then, around the end of the 18th century, as light brown *cassonade* (soft crystals). The final refining process to white crystals is usually carried out in European refineries.

The people of Guadeloupe consider sugar-cane cultivation to be their iron and steel industry. From February to June, the cane is harvested by hand, after the fields have been burned to rid them of snakes and dry undergrowth. Each cane is cut as close as possible to the ground, where the sugar content is the most concentrated. The cane is then tied into bundles and taken to the mill, where it is shredded then crushed under great rollers to extract the juice. This grey or dark green liquid is then fermented and distilled into rum, or evaporated and crystallized to make sugar. The dry residue is generally used for heating the boilers.

Northern Grande-Terre

On the east coast, **Porte d'Enfer** (Hell's Gate) is a strange fjord-like lagoon whose waters are delightful for bathing. A track leads up to the cliffs that guard its entrance. Beyond, **Pointe de la Grande Vigie** high above the ocean offers spectacular views.

On the road back to Pointe-à-Pitre, **Souffleur** beach at Port-Louis has gorgeous turquoise waters. At **Beauport**, **Le Pays de la Canne** is a sugar factory converted into a museum, where you can ride a little train through the cane fields. Stop off too at **Morne-à-l'Eau** to see the remarkable cemetery, its tombs completely covered with black and white chequerboard ceramics.

The vast bay of **Grand Cul-de-Sac Marin**, bordered by the longest coral reef of the Lesser Antilles, is hemmed in by mangrove swamps. They can be explored by boat or kayak and are rewarding for birdwatchers.

Basse-Terre

Columbus called it the Emerald Isle. Halted by the volcanic mass of La Soufrière, clouds empty over the land, watering the plentiful banana and coffee plantations and tropical forest. Along the coast, beaches and villages huddle in bays protected from the sometimes strong winds and hemmed in by coconut palms.

Northern Basse-Terre

The region is covered with fields of sugar cane and has several distilleries, as well as a **Musée du Rhum** (Reimonenq) which, in addition to displays on rum, shows exhibits of insects and models of sailing ships. Also in Sainte-Rose, the **Ecomusée Creole** explores traditional Creole culture and the island's flora, fauna and medicinal plants.

At **Deshaies**, the beautifully landscaped botanical garden is set in the grounds of a magnificent residence that belonged to the French comedian and actor Coluche (1944–86). The splendid beach of **Grande Anse** is just at the northern exit of the village.

At **Pointe Noire**, you can learn all about chocolate at the **Maison du Cacao**, and taste the products made on site .

Route de la Traversée

The only inland road, the D23, meanders through the Guadeloupe national park, a majestic forest of mahogany, ferns, lianas and orchids. **Cascade aux Ecrevisses** (Crayfish Falls) is a lovely picnic area where you can swim in the rocky, fern-carpeted pool beneath the waterfall.

A little further, the **Maison de la Forêt** is the departure point for forest trails into the **Parc National de la Guadeloupe**; it has an interesting exhibition devoted to nature.

Going down towards the west coast, the **Zoo Guadeloupe–Parc des Mamelles** houses Antilles wildlife and Guyanese species such as jaguars in a natural forest setting. Activities include a canopy walk and visits to an insectarium.

West Coast

Grey or brown sand and pebbles line the deep blue sea, as the road follows the contours of capes and bays, climbing and falling into flower-filled hamlets. From **Malendure Beach**, excursions can be arranged to **Pigeon Island**, and you can snorkel, dive or take glass-bottomed boat ride in the **Réserve Cousteau** offshore of Bouillante.

South of the reserve, **Vieux-Habitants** is home to two attractions themed around coffee: the **Musée du Café** centres on the history of coffee production in Guadeloupe, while the **Maison du Café** is a working plantation where you can see the process in action. At Saint-Claude, **La Bonifiere** is a cocoa plantation and chocolate factory open to visitors.

The little town of **Basse-Terre**, smaller and sleepier than Pointe-à-Pitre, may remind you of a French provincial town, bar its tropical seaside setting at the foot of La Soufrière's slopes. **Fort Delgrès**, situated at Brimstone Hill, dates from 1645, with superlative views and a small history museum.

La Soufrière

Temperamental and magnificent, even if its peak is almost always draped in clouds, La Soufrière is a semi-active volcano and the centrepoint of the Parc National de la Guadeloupe. From its height of 1,467 m, it dominates the lush and rugged south of Basse-Terre. La Soufrière last erupted in 1976 and is carefully monitored. You reach it via a winding road through the forest, starting at St-Claude and ending at **Bains Jaunes**, with a small thermal pool (27°C). From there it takes about an hour and a half to reach the summit.

Southern Tip

From Trois-Rivières, boats cross over to the islands of Les Saintes in under half an hour. Just below the port, the **Parc Archeologique des Roches Gravées** is a small botanical garden containing 230 ancient Arawak rock engravings.

After Bananier, an asphalted road leads into the eastern slopes of La Soufrière, passing through several plantations of tropical flowers and past a turnoff to the placid lake of **Grand Etang**, to the **Chutes du Carbet**. Two of these three delightful waterfalls, cascading amid a tangle of ferns and tree vines, can be viewed from a platform. The paths to the foot of the falls are often impassable after heavy rain.

East Coast

Before **Capesterre-Belle-Eau**, twin rows of majestic royal palms line the **Allée Dumanoir**, named after the man who planted them. Further north is a colourful **Hindu temple**, built by the descendants of Indian immigrants brought in to work the sugar plantations.

Sainte-Marie is the spot where Christopher Columbus landed in 1493, and his statue has pride of place in the village square. From Petit-Bourg, a short detour takes you to **Jardins de Valombreuse**, with a tropical flower park where hummingbirds feed, a water-playground and horse-riding.

Marie-Galante

Large and round, and noted for the rum from its extensive sugar-cane fields, Marie-Galante was named by Columbus after the ship that brought him across the Atlantic on his second voyage. The island has a number of fine white-sand beaches, notably **Moustique** and **Anse du Vieux Fort** both north of St-Louis, **La Feuillère** and **Petite Anse** near Capesterre. East of Grand Bourg, amid a former sugar plantation, the restored **Château Murat** has a museum and a garden of medicinal plants. The sugar mill at **Le Bézard** has been entirely restored. Visit the three old distilleries: **Poisson**, **Bielle** and **Bellevue**, where they claim to make the best rum in the world.

The spectacular waterfalls of Carbet, at the foot of the Soufrière, consist of three falls, the highest of which measures 115 m.

La Désirade

Beautiful beaches lure the determined few off the beaten track to La Désirade, with an area of only 21 sq km (8 sq miles). This was the first of the Antilles spotted by Columbus in 1493. A single road, 10 km (6 miles) long, links the three villages of **Grande Anse**, in the west, via **Le Souffleur** to the superb **Baie-Mahault** in the east. Its highest peak is **Grande Montagne**, at 280 m. The island has a wide range of flora and fauna.

With quaint villages and turquoise bays, Les Saintes slumbers under the tropical sun.

Les Saintes

The eight islands of Les Saintes form a miniature archipelago just 10 km (6 miles) south of Guadeloupe's Basse-Terre. Only two are inhabited, by descendants of the first Breton and Norman settlers. The islands were the scene of a great battle in 1782 when the English defeated the French.

Because the land was too arid for cultivation, the settlers turned to fishing, and now the Saintois are said to be the best sailors in the Antilles. Their distinctive, long keel-less boats, also called *saintois*, are used all around Guadeloupe, though their conical traditional straw hats, or *salako*, have been relegated to the realm of souvenirs.

The majority of the 3,000 inhabitants live on Terre-de-Haut, the smallest but also the loveliest of the islands.

Terre-de-Haut

Red-roofed houses nestle on the hills surrounding this pleasant, tourist-friendly municipality. The local people make a living from tourism and fishing. On the main square, a monument commemorates the French Revolution and the town hall flies a red, white and blue flag honouring the "mother country".

Fort Napoléon

Built in the 19th century, the fort was restored a few years ago and now houses an interesting museum with displays on local history. It is surrounded by a pretty gardens. Looking out over the north side of Terre-de-Haut it offers fine views of Guadeloupe and Marigot Bay to the east.

Beaches

Sheltered behind a rampart of eroded rocks, **Pompierre Bay** on the island's northeast coast has a magnificent sandy beach.

On the Atlantic coast, opposite Bourg des Saintes, **Grande Anse** is spectacular, but dangerous for swimming.

To the south, the **Pain de Sucre** (literally, Sugar Loaf) peninsula is rimmed by heavenly stretches of fine sand: **Anse Devant**, **Petite Anse** and **Anse à Coin**.

Anse Crawen further south offers the best snorkelling and skin diving.

Martinique

The Indians called it Madinina—island of flowers—and they were right: hibiscus and bougainvillaea, oleander, anthurium, poinsettia and more all compete to make Martinique one of the most colourful tropical gardens on earth.

When Columbus discovered the island, he called it "the best, most fertile, sweetest, most charming country in the world" and named it Matinino, probably after St Martin (or, some say, as an approximation of Madinina), a name which the French later adapted to Martinique.

Fort-de-France

Clinging to its superb harbour, Martinique's capital is sometimes bustling, sometimes drowsy—but always captivating. Awesome green mountains form the backdrop while strikingly tall palm trees dwarf most of the buildings.

La Savane

Visitors and Martiniquais alike tend to gravitate towards this landscaped park, near the water's edge in the heart of the city. Pierre Belain d'Esnambuc, the Norman adventurer who first claimed Martinique for France, has a statue here, cast in bronze. On the north side of the park a white marble statue of Napoleon's Josephine has been decapitated and splashed in red paint as a protest against her role in encouraging Napoleon to re-introduce slavery in 1802. The park also boasts snack shops and a tourist information office.

Alongside La Savane runs rue de la Liberté, and at No. 9 is the excellent **Musée Départemental**, documenting the island's pre-Columbian history. The collection of Arawak and Carib objects includes engraved cups and some remarkable decorative painted figurines known as *adornos*.

Town Centre

The teeming shopping area centres on the **Grand Marché** covered market between Antoine Siger and Blenac streets, overflowing with exotic fruit, vegetables, spices and souvenirs. If you are here early enough, go to the nearby **fish market** on the Madame River (Levassor canal). The **cruise terminal** is near the mouth of the channel, next to the bus station.

It's hard to miss the **Cathédrale St-Louis de Fort-de-France**, a vast metallic structure dating from 1895 and the last of seven churches to stand on this spot. Its architect, Henri Picq, also designed the startling **Bibliothèque Schoelcher** on rue de la Liberté, a strange blend of Byzantine and contemporary that was originally at the World's Fair, then dismantled and shipped to Martinique.

For an unrivalled view of the town, climb up to the **Chapelle du Calvaire** through the Didier residential district with its handsome colonial houses.

West Coast

Take a stroll around **Case-Pilote**, one of the oldest villages on Martinique, which boasts a venerable baroque church built of stone in the centre, and an enchanting main square complete with fountain and elegant town hall.

Joséphine. Marie-Josèphe Rose Tascher de La Pagerie was born on June 23, 1763, at the Petite Guinée, her parents' plantation. Aged 16, she set sail for France where she married the son of a former governor of the Windward Isles, Viscount de Beauharnais. Two children were born, Eugène and Hortense, but the marriage was not a happy one and finally Marie-Josèphe returned to Martinique. In 1790, during the Terror, her husband was guillotined. Back in France, in 1796 she remarried a promising army general, six years younger than herself: Napoleon Bonaparte, who called her Joséphine. In 1809, Emperor Napoleon repudiated her, as she had not given him a successor.

The large town of **Le Carbet**, where Columbus and Belain d'Esnambuc disembarked, owes its name to the original settlement founded by Amerindians. Nowadays the family-owned **Neisson Distillery**, which produces a tasty rum, attracts plenty of visitors.

One of the island's oldest buildings, the Habitation Anse Latouche was destroyed by Mont Pelée's 1902 eruption. Surrounded by lovely gardens, its ruins are now the centrepiece of the small **Zoo Martinique**, whose residents include kangaroos, howler monkeys and jaguars.

Further north at Anse Turin, the **Paul Gauguin Interpretive Centre** is dedicated to the famous French artist, who stayed here in 1887. Currently undergoing refurbishment, it's due to reopen in 2015.

St-Pierre

Once a lovely seaside town, St-Pierre was the first French settlement on Martinique. When 1,397-m Mont Pelée, an active volcano, began to belch smoke and cinders far above the town on April 24, 1902, authorities professed no concern. Evacuation was unthinkable — an election was coming up. On May 5, a mass of mud and rocks was swept down by Pelée's White River (Rivière Blanche), destroying the Guérin sugar factory and killing 25 people, while a tidal wave

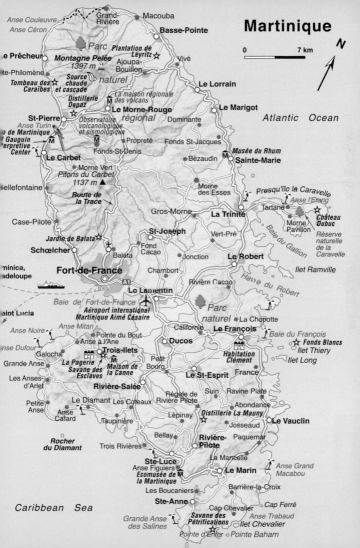

Martinique

N

0   7 km

Anse Couleuvre
Anse Céron
Grand-
Rivière
Macouba
Basse-Pointe
Parc
Montagne Pelée *Plantation de*
Le Prêcheur *Leyritz*
1397 m
ste-Philomène *Ajoupa-*
Tombeau des **Source** *Bouillon* Vivé
Caraïbes **chaude** *naturel* **Le Lorrain**
et cascade
Distillerie *La maison régionale* **Le Marigot**
Anse Turin **Depaz** *des volcans*
St-Pierre M **Le Morne-**
o de Martinique *Observatoire* **Rouge**
Gauguin *volcanologique* *régional*
rprétive *et sismologique* Dominante
Center M **Propreté** Fonds St-Jacques
Le Carbet *Musée du Rhum*
Bézaudin M **Sainte-Marie**
Morne Vert
Pitons du Carbet *Morne*
1137 m *des Esses*
Presqu'île la Caravelle
ellefontaine *Route de* *Anse l'Étang*
la Trace Gros-Morne **La Trinité** Tartane
Case-Pilote **Château**
Morne *Dubuc*
Pavillon
St-Joseph Vert-Pré *Réserve*
Jardin de Balata *naturelle*
de la
Schœlcher *Caravelle*
Balata Jonction **Le Robert**
Fond
Cacao *Îlet Ramville*
Fort-de-France Chambort
A1 *Havre du Robert*
Lo Lamentin Rivière Cacao
Baie de Fort-de-France *Parc*
minica, *Aéroport international* *naturel*
deloupe *Martinique Aimé Césaire* Californie **La Chapotte**
Le François *Baie du François*
Anse Mitan **Fonds Blancs**
aint Lucia *Pointe du Bout* **Ducos** *Îlet Thiery*
Anse Noire *Anse à l'Âne* *Îlet Long*
Habitation
nse Dufour *Trois-Îlets* **Clément**
Galocha M Petit France
La Pagerie *Bourg* **Le St-Esprit**
Grande Anse *Savane des*
Esclaves Maison
Les Anses- *de la Canne*
d'Arlet **Rivière-Salée** Régale de
Suin *Rivière Pilote* Ravine Plate
Petite **Le Diamant** Les Coteaux Abondance
Anse *Anse* Lépinay **Distillerie La Mauny** **Le Vauclin**
Cafard Josseaud
Taupinière Bellay Paquemar
Rocher Trois Rivières **Rivière-**
du Diamant **Pilote**
La Manzelle *Anse Grand*
Ste-Luce *Macabou*
Le Marin
Écomusée de M
la Martinique Barrière-la-Croix
Les Boucaniers
Ste-Anne Cap Chevalier Cap Ferré
Savane des *Anse Trabaud*
Caribbean Sea *Grande Anse* *Pétrifications* *Îlet Chevalier*
des Salines
Pointe d'Enfer Pointe Baham

Atlantic Ocean

Baie du Galion

lashed the shores near St-Pierre. Flames began spouting from the mountain's peak, and residents began to panic. On May 7 the governor of Martinique arrived with his wife to reassure the population, but during the night of the 7th and 8th, a huge wave of mud swept over the villages of the north coast. But the authorities remained blind to the danger and persuaded the people to stay calm. At precisely 7.52 a.m on May 9th, the volcano erupted. A burning cloud of gas and steam bearing rocks, lava and ashes roared down the mountainside onto the town, and in just 3 minutes, St-Pierre was totally wiped out. There were only two or three survivors, including a certain Cyparis, prisoner in a thick-walled dungeon. For years afterwards he was displayed abroad as an attraction of Barnum circus. Less than three months later, another eruption destroyed the eastern slope of the volcano, killing a thousand.

The eruption is documented in the **Musée municipal Vulcanologique et Historique Franck Perret**, where old photographs and postcards show the town as it was before disaster struck, alongside pieces of molten glass, twisted metal and burnt food that illustrate the wreckage. You can walk through the ruined town and see the church, fort, theatre with behind it the prison that saved the life of Cyparis. You can also tour St-Pierre's sights on the **Cyparis Express**, a miniature tourist train.

At the north exit of town, the **Centre de Découverte des Sciences de la Terre (CDST)** is also devoted to Mont Pelée, with displays on the volcano and videos documenting the 1902 eruption.

Founded in the 17th century, the **Distillerie Depaz** was destroyed in the eruption. The rum factory was re-opened in 1917 and the plantation house rebuilt in 1922. Today 250 tonnes of sugar cane are processed here every day, in season, producing 25,000 litres of rum. Self-guided tours are available, as are rum-tastings.

Mancenillier. Native to the West Indies, the small mancenillier or manchineel tree *(Hyppomane mancenilla)* which grows on the beaches, is extremely dangerous. Its white, milky sap contains Prussic acid—a violent poison—in sufficient quantity to burn anyone who comes into contact with it. Even rainwater dripping from the branches can burn holes in clothing. The fruit resemble crab apples but are also toxic.

fotolia.com/Perinelle

ATTENTION MANCENILLIER ARBRE TOXIQUE · MIND MANCHINEEL POISONOUS TREE

Northern Beaches

The **Tombeau des Caraïbes** is where the last Indians of Martinique are said to have jumped to their deaths to escape enslavement.

The old village of **Le Prêcheur**, fringed by rubber trees along the shore, was the childhood home of Françoise d'Aubigné, who later in life became Madame de Maintenon, the wife of Louis XIV.

The road goes on to **Anse Céron**, a superb beach shaded by coconut palms, then ends a few kilometres further on as it approaches **Anse Couleuvre**, a carpet of black sand lined by majestic coconut palms. A footpath leads through the tropical forest to **Grand-Rivière**, a fishing village 18 km (11 miles) away at the northern tip of the island.

Route de la Trace

The Jesuits opened this road from Fort-de-France through the forest in the 17th century. Emerging from the vegetation, **Balata church** is a miniaturized replica of the Sacré-Cœur basilica in Paris. A little further, at the foot of the Carbet peaks *(pitons)*, the **Jardin de Balata** displays over a thousand labelled varieties of tropical plants and flowers, whose nectar attracts a dazzling array of hummingbirds. The well-marked path through includes wooden walkways set some 500 feet up in the air, which afford lovely views of the gardens below.

The road takes you to Morne-Rouge at the foot of Mont Pelée. The volcano has shown no sign of erupting since the 1930s, but its activity is closely monitored the **L'Observatoire Volcanologique et Sismologique de Martinique**, a scientific facility that is closed to the public. Hikers can attempt the strenuous walk up to the summit; trails start from Morne-Rouge and Grand-Rivière.

Atlantic Coast

The northeast of the island was destroyed by Hurricane Dean in 2007 and several sites suffered extensive damage, like the famous **Leyritz Plantation**. Rebuilding of the vast estate, created around 1700, is ongoing and it remains closed to the public.

At **Fonds St-Jacques**, the Dominican monastery was founded in 1659 and was the most important industrial centre of the island. It was here that Father Labat devised the "cognac" method of distilling rum. The site is now home to the **Domaine de Saint-Jacques** arts and culture centre.

At St James Distillery in Sainte-Marie, the **Musée du Rhum** traces the history of sugar cane and the national drink, while distillery tours explain the art of rum-making and offer a tasting session. Nearby **Morne-des-Esses** is noted for its basketwork crafted in the Carib tradition.

DINING AND SHOPPING

On the menu

Martinique and Guadeloupe are both famed for their cuisine, some of the best in the Caribbean. The food of the Antilles is a happy blend of influences from all its colourful population—French, African, Indian—and uses the freshest of ingredients. *Accras* are fritters of cod, sea urchins, vegetables or meat. *Blaff* is fish or shellfish marinated in a mixture of lime juice, garlic and spices then simmered in stock. Little octopus, *chatroux*, are generally stewed. *Dombrés*, pork meatballs, are served with red beans. You must try *matoutou* or *matété de crabes*, land crabs sautéed with garlic and onions, seasoned with lemon juice, thyme and hot pepper. *Pâté en pot* hovers somewhere between a soup and a stew: it generally includes mutton offal, bacon and ham, flavoured with cloves and bay leaves. *Z'habitants* are big crayfish from fast-running rivers, cooked in a spicy stock.

In the markets you'll have noticed the abundance of tropical fruit. Coconut tart is delectable. You will also find a wide selection of fruit sorbets.

Rum, with a measure of cane syrup and a zest of lime, becomes a *ti-punch*, everyone's favourite afternoon drink.

The best buys

Local craftsmen produce attractive pottery, and you will find brightly coloured sarongs, dolls in madras costumes, straw dolls, and beautiful Creole jewellery.

On the market stalls, you will see headily perfumed vanilla in many forms—plaited pods, essence, etc., and all kinds of spices wrapped in small bags. Among them is the famous aphrodisiac, *bois bandé*. And don't forget a bottle of rum. The best island rums have been aged in barrels for at least 15 years.

St. Barts is famed for its luxury tax-free shopping, with designer boutiques lining the Rue de la République in Gustavia.

flickr.com/Chardon

Part of the **Parc Naturel Régional de la Martinique**, the Caravelle peninsula supports a wealth of wildlife, best seen via two walking trails. At its northern end, explore the lovely beaches of **Tartane** and **Anse l'Etang** and the ruins of the 17th-century **Château Dubuc**. Further south, **Baie du Robert**, dotted with tiny isles, is superb for boat or kayak trips over the white sands around the reefs. Just off **Le François**, you can picnic and swim at the **Fonds Blancs** sandbanks, also known as "Joséphine's Bath".

Inland, the **Habitation Clément** is an 18th-century mansion furnished in antiques, and with a distillery famous for its aged rum. Tours cover the house and art gallery, the beautifully landscaped gardens and the rum factory.

The South

Joséphine, wife of Napoleon and Empress of France, was born at a sugar estate in **Trois Ilets**, south of Fort-de-France. The tiny **Musée de la Pagerie** here displays her childhood bed and other memorabilia.

On Trois Islets' main square, the church of **L'Eglise Notre Dame de la Bonne Déliverance** holds the font where Joséphine was baptised.

Look in too at the **Maison de la Canne**, devoted to the history of sugar-cane production; and the interactive **Savane des Esclaves**, which explores slavery and life on the plantations.

The famous Diamond Rock was elevated to the status of a ship.

Pointe-du-Bout, with its marina and hotels, is the biggest resort of the island. Continue to the grey-sand beach of Anse à l'Ane, then **Anse Noire** and **Anse Dufour**, two neighbouring beaches, one with white sand and coconut palms.

After **Les Anses d'Arlet** you'll suddenly be confronted by a gigantic bulk rising up out of the sea. **Diamond Rock** (Rocher du Diamant) was occupied by the Royal Navy as a strategic base during the struggle for Martinique in 1804. Officially elevated to the rank of a ship, *H.M.S. Diamond Rock* bombarded French positions and ships for 18 months.

The **Trois Rivières Distillery** is not in active production, but you can take a tour and buy some rum.

From Sainte-Luce onwards, one lovely beach succeeds another as far as **Sainte-Anne**, one of the main resorts. Its best-known beach is **Les Salines**.

THE HARD FACTS

Airport. Guadeloupe: Pôle Caraïbes (PTP), 3 km (2 miles) from Point-à-Pitre; Martinique: Aimé Cesarie (FDF) in Le Lamentin, 11 km (7 miles) from Fort-de-France; St-Barthélemy: Gustaf III (SBH) in St-Jean, around 1km (0.6 miles) from Gustavia. Inter-island flights serve Grande-Case airport on Saint-Martin, and there are several flights daily between Guadeloupe and Les Saintes, Marie-Galante and La Désirade.

Climate. Winter is the dry season; summer is hotter and wetter. Rainfall is heavier from mid-June to mid-August and October to November. On the coast, average temperatures range from 25°C to 30°C, day and night.

Clothing. Take lightweight clothes and a warm sweater for cool evenings and trips into the mountains. Don't wander around towns in beachwear.

Driving. Speed limits are 120 kph on motorways, 50 kph in built-up areas and 90 kph on other roads, except in St-Barthélemy where the limit on all roads is 45 kph.

Electricity. 220 volts 50/60 Hz.

Language. French is spoken on all the French islands, but Creole is preferred in private; English is understood in touristic areas. English is the main language of Anguilla, Antigua and Barbuda and Montserrat.

Money. Guadeloupe, Martinique, St-Barthélemy and St-Martin use the Euro; Anguilla, Antigua and Barbuda and Montserrat use the EC dollar. Credit cards and US dollars are widely accepted. There are ATMs in all the main towns.

Time. UTC/GMT −4, all year round.

Tipping. It is usual to leave a tip equivalent to 10 percent of the bill.

Water. Bottled mineral water is widely available and is advised.

Transport. There are plenty of local buses and collective taxis. Private taxis are metered, but can be very expensive. Fares go up by fifty percent on Sundays and holidays.

St Kitts and Nevis

Luscious vegetation in all its tropical brilliance, coconut palms stretching along white- or black-sand beaches and mist-shrouded volcanic mountain peaks make St Kitts and Nevis one of the most desirable resort areas in the Caribbean. The islands remain largely unspoiled, thanks to a sensible policy of controlled development.

St Kitts

When Columbus discovered the larger island in 1493, he was so taken with it that he named it after himself. Sir Thomas Warner took one look at St Christopher 130 years later and dubbed it a cosier, British "St Kitts", a name that stuck from that day to this.

Basseterre

The lively little capital is home to around 15,500 people, roughly half of the total population of 32,000. The bustling port hums with activity as boats of every description come and go. Only two ships at a time can moor at the cruise dock; the others are served by tenders. A colourful market is held in Basseterre, a mosaic of exotic sights and smells, while the **National Museum**

The mountains of St Kitts often wear a cloak of mist. | Basseterre's Circus and its eye-catching clocktower.

Claude Hervé-Bazin

Huber/Gräfenhain

ST KITTS AND NEVIS FLASHBACK

15th–17th centuries
Columbus discovers St Kitts (and sights Nevis) in 1493; he names it St Christopher after himself (and his patron saint). Sir Thomas Warner lands there with his wife, son and a party of thirteen on January 28, 1623, and changes the name to the cosier St Kitts. A hurricane destroys the first tobacco crop in September of the same year. Sir Thomas and Pierre Belain d'Esnambuc of France conclude a treaty (1627) for division of the island, as well as a mutual defence pact against the Spaniards and Carib Indians. Warner starts a settlement on Nevis in 1628. Belain d'Esnambuc attacks the English in 1629 and regular skirmishes between the two occur over the course of the next seven years. Sir Thomas Warner dies in 1648.

18th century
Britain gains St Kitts under terms of the Treaty of Utrecht (1713); the French attack and capture Brimstone Hill Fort in 1782, but return it to the British the following year, as stipulated by the Treaty of Versailles.

19th century
Slaves are emancipated in 1834, but no equitable redistribution of land takes place. The islands of St Kitts, Nevis and Anguilla are united in 1882.

20th century–present
St Kitts-Nevis-Anguilla is established as an independent state in association with Great Britain in 1967. The same year Anguilla seeks independence from St Kitts and is restored to colonial status in 1971. St Kitts and Nevis gain full independence in 1983. The economy flourishes with the development of tourism and the export of sugar, cotton, coconuts and citrus fruit. The state-owned sugar company is closed down in 2005; many cane fields are burned to make room for land development.

Claude Hervé-Bazin

St Kitts and Nevis

St Paul's Point

Dieppe Bay
Parsons Ground
St Paul's
Sadlers
Newton Ground

St Kitts

andy Point
Tabernacle
Mansion

UNESCO World Heritage Site
Mt Liamuiga 1156 m
Molineux
Grange Bay

mp ay

Brimstone Hill Fort National Park
Philips
Lodge

Half Way Tree
Godwin Ghut
Middle Island

Ottley's Ghut
Cayon

Romney Manor
Wingfield Petroglyphs
South East Range 900 m
Key's

Old Road Town

Stapleten

Bloody Point
Challengers
Monkey Hill
Upper Conaree

Palmetto Bay
St Kitts Scenic Railway
Robert L. Bradshaw International Airport

Palmetto Point

BASSETERRE
Half Moon Bay
Muddy Point
Royal St. Kitts Golf Club

Port Zante
North Frigate Bay

Atlantic Ocean

Frigate Bay
North Friar's Bay

South Frigate Bay
South Friar's Bay

Sand Bank Bay

Ballast Bay
Great Salt Pond
St Anthony's Peak 319 m
Mosquito Bluff
Turtle Beach
Mosquito Bay

Nag's Head
Banana Bay

Narrows

Caribbean Sea

Windy Hill Point
Lovers Beach
Vance W. Amory International Airport

The
Oualie Beach
Newcastle

Cades Bay
Scarborough
Brick Kiln

Cotton Ground
Westbury
Mannings

Pinney's Beach
Vaughans

Nevis

Fountain Ghut

Alexander Hamilton Museum
Museum of Nevis History
Nevis Peak 985 m

Charlestown
Craddocks
Zetlands
Zion

Fort Charles
Horatio Nelson Museum
Market Shop
Nevisian Heritage Village

Bath

Figtree
Holmes Hill

Brown Hill
Botanical Gardens of Nevis

Pembroke

N

0   5 km

in the domed former Treasury Building gives the lowdown on local history. With its Victorian **clocktower**, **The Circus** square is the heart of Basseterre. The around **Fort Street** and **Independence Square** abounds in shops, cafés and colonial buildings such as the imposing **Immaculate Conception Cathedral**.

Just outside town, **Clay Villa Plantation House** dates back to 1763. You can explore the 4 ha (10 acre) gardens, replete with fruit trees and flowers, and tour the house, decorated in period style and home to a history museum

Around St Kitts

Most visitors soon head out of Basseterre for a round-the-island tour. Going clockwise, the road leads into vast stretches of old sugar cane and cotton plantations.

St Kitts Scenic Railway

Originally built to transport sugar cane from field to factory, the narrow-gauge railway has been converted into a visitor attraction and is a great way to see the main sights and some ravishing coastline. Departing from just outside Basseterre, the carriages have an open-sided upper deck and an air-conditioned lower one. Guides point out highlights such as Brimstone Hill and give a commentary on St Kitts' history. Note that 45 minutes of the trip is by road rather than rail.

Wingfield Estate, Romney Manor

Just above Road Town, a pretty little village which once served as the island's capital, the dilapidated Wingfield Estate was once home to a rum distillery. Today, you can walk trails through the grounds to see Amerindian petroglyphs and the crumbling estate buildings, or try ziplining with **Sky Safari**. Historic Romney Manor is home to **Caribelle Batik**, where you can watch artists creating colourful pieces, and tour the pretty gardens, home to a 350-year-old saman tree.

Brimstone Hill Fort National Park

A UNESCO World Heritage site, the massive construction, said to have taken 100 years to build, mainly from local volcanic stone, must surely be one of the wonders of the Caribbean. It was from these majestic battlements, 213 m up, that the British picked off the French galleons with pinpoint accuracy during the many 17th- and 18th-century battles for the island. But the British were not always invincible. In the 1782 Battle of Brimstone Hill, the French won a gallant victory and, for a while, the tricolor flag flew from the warped and battle-scarred fortifications.

The **DL Matheson Visitor Centre** presents a video introducing the fort, and there's an interesting museum in the barrack rooms.

Dieppe Bay Town

This resort is of interest mainly to visitors in search of peace and quiet. Good hotels and a pleasant beach make it a popular stop-off before heading south through former sugar plantations.

Frigate Bay

Southeast of Basseterre near the fairways of the 18-hole championship golf course, Frigate Bay is home to hotels, bars and a popular white-sand beach.

Nevis

Nevis lies 3 km (2 miles) south of St Kitts, across the strip of water known as The Narrows, 45 minutes by fast ferry from Basseterre. The island has good hotels, magnificent beaches, friendly people, and an intriguing past.

Charlestown

This pretty little waterfront capital, its buildings fronted by elaborate balconies and gingerbread fretwork, is home to the old **Bath Hotel and Springs**, a fashionable spot during the 19th century. The hotel is now the local government headquarters, but you can still bathe in the restorative spring waters.

Horatio Nelson Museum

Nearby, this small collection of artefacts celebrate the famous admiral, who married Fanny Nisbet in Nevis.

Museum of Nevis History, Alexander Hamilton Birthplace

Destined to become one of America's most outstanding statesmen, Alexander Hamilton was born in Charlestown on January 11, 1757, the son of Rachel Lavien of Nevis and a Scottish adventurer, James Hamilton. In 1765 James abandoned his family in St Croix. His mother died in 1768, leaving young Alexander entirely on his own. Through perseverance and hard work he went on to become Secretary of the Treasury in George Washington's cabinet, and helped to draft the US Constitution. He died after a duel on July 11, 1804. Today, the charming cut-stone house in which he was born is home to the **Museum of Nevis History**. Displays explore Hamilton's life as well as providing the lowdown on local events.

St John's Figtree Anglican Church

Inland of Charlestown, Nelson's marriage certificate is displayed at the church where he was married. It was built in 1680 and twice restored in the 19th century. The register contains the signatures of the happy couple.

Botanical Gardens of Nevis

Figtree Parish is also home to these charming gardens, lush with tropical flora, from bromeliads and orchids to over 100 varieties of palm tree.

Dominica

Dominicans call their island the land of the three R's: rivers, rainbows and romance. And that's no exaggeration. Some 365 rivers, one for every day of the year, tumble and cascade through the forest, and rainbows dance over the waterfalls. As for romance, Dominica can certainly lay claim to being the most ruggedly beautiful of the Caribbean islands, with a mystique that hangs in the air like the perennial fine mist that the islanders term "liquid sunshine".

At the northern end of the Windward chain, the island measures 47 km (29 miles) in length and 26 km (16 miles) wide at the broadest part. A mountainous chain runs from north to south, rising to 1,447 m Morne Diablotin (Devil Mountain).

Roseau

The capital and main port lies in the delta of the Roseau River on the southwest coast. Many of the old colonial buildings have been restored to their former Caribbean charm. But most of the town is a jumble of one- or two-storey structures with ironwork balconies overhanging the pavements. Along the river banks, you'll see the profusion of reeds which gave the town its name. The Caribs used them to make poison-tipped arrows, and they are now essential to the basket-making industry. **Bay Front** runs along the harbour, and cruise ships dock near the **Old Market Square**, originally built to house slave auctions and now filled with crafts stalls. Just opposite is the small **Dominica Museum**, with displays centred on the island's history and traditions.

Inland, one of the oldest buildings in Roseau is **Government House**, dating back to the 1840s. Wander through the labyrinth of streets to the **Cathedral of Our Lady of Fair Haven** (1854), whose carved wooden benches are more than 100 years old. One of the stained-glass windows in the side walls depicts Columbus's voyage to the Americas.

Morne Bruce

Behind the town rises the peak of Morne Bruce, the summit affording a good view back over Roseau and the harbour. You can reach it by car along a twisting road or climb the footpath from the **Botanic Gardens** on the southern edge of town. The gardens provide a splendid introduction to the island's flora, from orchids and flame trees to medicinal plants. Look out, too, for the twisted remains of a school bus, crushed by a baobab tree during Hurricane Davis in 1979. There's also an aviary where the endangered Sisserou and Jaco parrots are bred.

Champagne Reef

South of Roseau, this remarkable spot is named for the bubbles of gas which ripple up through the water here. You can rent a snorkel and mask and explore the off-shore reefs and marine life.

Soufriere Sulphur Springs

These bubbling pools of grey mud belch out sulphurous fumes that give off a pungent rotten-egg smell. Nearby **Scott's Head** is a picturesque fishing beach.

Interior

Any point on the island is only a comfortable day-trip away, while the interior promises hikes through pristine rainforest.

Trafalgar Falls

Situated 8 km (5 miles) northeast of the capital, Trafalgar Falls can be reached by car to the village of Trafalgar, and then by a 15-minute walk. In a setting of dripping greenery, hot and cold cascades crash and splash into a rocky pool sprouting ferns and orchids. An observation platform gives optimal viewing.

The nearby **Papillote Wilderness Retreat** is a nature sanctuary and a paradise for birdwatchers, with 150 colourful species of bird flitting around the ferns and orchids of the garden. Non-guests are able to explore the garden's labyrinth of paths.

hemis.fr/Gardel

Traditional houses in Roseau boast cheerfully painted façades and louvred blinds at the windows.

Morne Trois Pitons National Park

You can reach the park, a UNESCO World Heritage site, via three distinct routes. The **Laudat Village** road takes you to the departure point of several marked nature trails, the most popular of which lead to Freshwater Lake, Boeri Lake and Boiling Lake. In the lush, dense undergrowth, the plants and trees are labelled for easy identification. The trek to Freshwater Lake is uphill: it lies at 1,100 m, its surface dappled with purple water hyacinths. From a grassy knoll,

DOMINICA FLASHBACK

Pre-Columbian era
Carib Indians migrate to the Antilles from the South American mainland and settle on Dominica, ousting the peaceful Arawaks. On Sunday, November 3, 1493, Christopher Columbus sights the island and names it Dominica.

17th–18th centuries
British and French try to settle here in the 17th century, fiercely resisted by the Caribs. With the 1748 Treaty of Aix-la-Chapelle, Britain and France agree to leave Dominica as neutral territory, in the possession of the Caribs. Nonetheless, the fertile soil attracts both French and British planters who attempt to establish themselves. The Peace of Paris in 1763 formally gives Dominica to the British, but the island continues to be juggled between the colonial powers.

19th century–present
In 1805 the French burn down the capital, Roseau, and relinquish their hold on the island only upon payment of £8,000. Between 1833 and 1940, Dominica is governed by the British as part of the Leeward Islands, then it is transferred to the Windward Islands as a separate colony.

In November, 1978, Dominica gains full independence within the Commonwealth. Hurricanes in 1979 and 1980 leave despair and destruction, with 60,000 homeless and the largely agricultural economy in disarray. But Dominica rebuilds, developing its tourist trade with a special emphasis on its unique attractions. Today the population numbers 70,000 (in great majority the descendants of slaves).

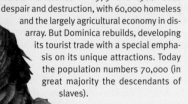

Corbis/Huey

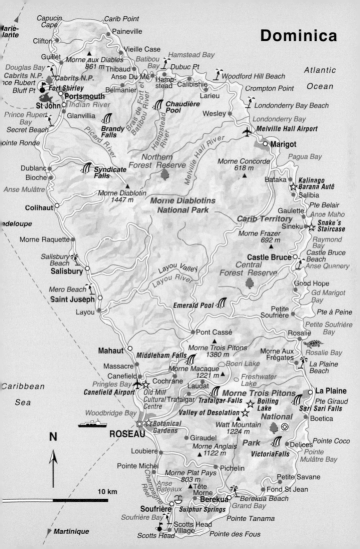

you have a magnificent view of the Atlantic on one side and the Caribbean on the other. The Boeri Lake trail starts at the shores of the reservoir. At an altitude of 853 m, the lake is almost circular in shape, with a rocky shoreline.

Much more challenging is the rough 9-km (6-mile) track to the **Valley of Desolation**, taking three or four hours one-way. The area lives up to its name with a stark landscape stripped of its vegetation by volcanic upheavals, the last major one in 1880.

The eruption created the **Boiling Lake**, which geologists believe is a flooded crack in the earth (fumarole) rather than a volcanic crater. Escaping gases from molten lava beneath the lake bring the water temperature to between 180 and 197 °F (82 and 92°C) at the edge and to boiling point in the middle. A cloud of steamy vapour hangs suspended over the lake.

Other Natural Wonders

To the northwest, Cochrane Village road runs past the trailhead to **Middleham Falls**, which shoot down into a clear, round pool. The 45 minute hike to the falls passes the aptly named **Stinking Hole**, a deep crevice that's home to thousands of bats.

From the Pont Cassé to Castle Bruce road, an easy trail leads to the ethereal **Emerald Pool**, a delightful grotto fed by a clear waterfall plunging over the edge of a fern-clad cliff. This northern section of the national park is also the start of climbs to the summit of **Morne Trois Pitons** (1,400 m).

North of Roseau, the **valley of Layou River** has been densely cultivated with a profusion of crops. Look out for plantations of grapefruit, banana, limes, tobacco and cocoa. The river is Dominica's longest; tubing excursions are organized.

West Coast

The coast road runs north from Roseau to the island's second town, Portsmouth. The scenic drive is both exhilarating and heart-stopping, punctuated by hairpin bends, steep gradients and tunnels, with spectacular views round every turn.

Portsmouth

Gaily painted wooden houses with flower-filled gardens line the streets that run parallel to **Prince Rupert Bay**. South of town you can take a trip along **Indian River**, gliding in a dugout canoe through past the twisted mangrove swamps, tracing the routed used by the Caribs from the sea to their settlements. More recently, the river provided a suitably eerie backdrop for scenes from the Pirates of the Caribbean movie *Dead Man's Chest*, much of which was filmed in Dominica.

Cabrits National Park

The peninsula jutting into the sea between Douglas and Prince Rupert bays holds the ruins of 18th-century **Fort Shirley**. The complex, restored as a museum, contains a hospital, barracks, store-houses, lookout posts and batteries, with a few cannon still facing out to sea. The whole area, endowed with tropical dry woodlands, freshwater swamps, marine reserve, and laced with hiking trails, makes up the **Cabrits National Park**. Established in 1986, the park occupies 531 ha (1,313 acres).

Northern Tip

Dominica's northern tip is dominated by the 861 m (2,824 ft) **Morne aux Diables**, while its coastline holds a host of pretty fishing villages such as **Calibishie**, where colourful boats pull up on the main beach and swimmers frolic at **Batibou Bay**.

East Coast

The Atlantic coast has a wild, untamed aspect, with beaches of pebbles or black sand, reddish cliffs dropping sheer into the sea and tropical vegetation crowding down to the water's edge.

Melville Hall Airport

The island's main airport, Melville Hall is linked to **Roseau** on the west coast by a road cut through the mountain interior.

The coastal road from the airport takes you further north to a string of gold-sand beaches, best of which is **Pagua Bay**, or south through several communities where fishermen bring in their catch, mend nets and build traditional canoes on the beach.

Carib Territory

Numbering some 3,000, the descendants of the island's original Carib inhabitants now live in a fertile 1,497-ha (3,700-acre) stretch of land running inland from the coast. The main destination is **Kalinago Barana Autê**, a recreated Carib village where guided tours offer a fascinating insight into their way of life. Highlights include a dugout canoe carved from a single tree-trunk, and a thatch-roofed *karbet*, used for cultural performances. Beautiful basketry is available in the craft shop. At **Touna Kalinago Heritage Village** in Concord, you can visit residential homes and see people engaged in basketry or making traditional foods such as cassava bread, also sold at the roadside Cassava Bakery in **Salybia**.

The serpentine shape of a solidified stream of lava protruding into the sea at **Sineku** has earned it the name **Snake Staircase** (L'escalier Tête-Chien). According to Carib legend, it marks the path taken by giant snake as it emerged from the ocean.

St Lucia

This appealing island midway between Martinique and St Vincent boasts some of the best scenery in the Caribbean: rugged green jungles, undulating agricultural terrain, dazzling beaches and the spectacular cone-shaped Pitons, twin volcanic spires that were declared a UNESCO World Heritage site in 2004. There's even a dormant but still bubbling volcano called Soufrière which you can drive right through without any danger. Francophiles love St Lucia for its French atmosphere. Many place-names are French—from the capital, Castries, to Vieux Fort on the southern tip of the island. The official language is English, but most of the 177,000 inhabitants also speak French patois, a remnant of the days of French colonization. Tourism is fairly well developed, but the island remains essentially agricultural, with bananas the main crop. There are provisions for all sorts of summer sports, and you can enjoy good music every night.

Castries

The island capital was named in 1785 after Maréchal de Castries, Minister of the Marine responsible for the French colonies. Few buildings remain from the 18th century, mainly due to devastating fires which swept the town in 1948 and 1951. Today's city of around 68,000 inhabitants looks jumbled, though some quarters have retained a certain charm.

Harbour

Take a look at the scenic yacht basin and the lively, ultra-modern **Pointe Seraphine** and **La Place Carenage** duty-free shopping complexes.

Just across the way, the **Central Market** hums with activity in the morning. You'll see plenty of island produce for sale, the array varying with the season, as well as lots of local craftwork, particularly straw goods.

Town Centre

On **Bridge Street** you'll find the central post office and the largest shops. **Derek Walcott Square**, one of the capital's few picturesque corners, has a central bandstand and a saman or rain tree which has been providing shade for four centuries. The square is named after the 1992 Nobel Prize winner for Literature, who still has a house on St Lucia, near Pigeon Island.

The Catholic **Cathedral of the Immaculate Conception** (19th-century) has wooden columns, iron vaulting and frescoes by the famous St Lucian artist Sir Dunstan St Omer (1927–2015).

Opposite stands a red and white structure in stucco and stone, the **Central Library**, surely the most handsome building in town. It was built in the 19th century but looks much older, and was funded by the Carnegie Trust.

Morne Fortune

Rising up behind the capital, the precipitous "Lucky Hill" is topped by **Fort Charlotte**, its 18th-century military buildings surrounded by sweeping lawns which offer spectacular views of the surrounding coastline. Both the French and the British conducted their squabbles from here, and the **Inniskilling Monument** commemorates the British capture of Morne Fortune in 1796.

The complex is also home to the St Lucian campus of the **University of the West Indies**, while three attractive 19th-century buildings hold part of the **Sir Arthur Lewis Community College**, named for the local academic who won the 1979 Nobel Prize for Economics.

On the way up to the fort, take a glance at **Government House**, an attractive Victorian building and the residence of the Governor General. Nearby, a roadside viewpoint affords sweeping vistas of Castries harbour.

The North

North of Castries lies the island's main resort area, **Rodney Bay**, spreading back from the lovely **Reduit Beach** and close to the fishing community of **Gros Islet**, best known for its Friday-night "jump-up", with live music and stalls selling local seafood.

On the way, the road passes golden-sand beach of **Choc Bay**.

istockphoto.com/Wildroze

The conical Pitons are St Lucia's most spectacular landmarks.

Pigeon Island National Landmark

Linked to the mainland by a causeway, this remarkable island of high green hills is a national park and a popular recreation spot, providing a spectacular setting for St Lucia's annual Jazz Festival each May. Used by Admiral Rodney as his headquarters in the 18th century, it was also a former pirate hideout. Island history is traced at the **Pigeon Island Museum**, set in the former Officer's Mess, while trails lead up the fortified hilltops to reveal fabulous coastal views.

ST LUCIA FLASHBACK

17th century

Early in the 17th century, a group of Englishmen from a ship called *The Olive Branch* attempts to set up a permanent colony; most are killed by Carib Indians within a few weeks. Efforts by both the British and French to colonize the island prove abortive until the second half of the century.

18th century

Strategically placed, St Lucia continues to tempt the British and French; the island changes hands between them more than a dozen times. In 1765, under the French, the first sugar plantation is started, small towns spring up and the island begins to prosper. But as the repercussions of the American and French revolutions spread to the West Indies, the battle between French and British for Caribbean supremacy intensifies.

19th century

The Treaty of Amiens awards St Lucia to France in 1802. The last transfer of power at the end of the Napoleonic Wars leaves St Lucia in British hands. The 19th century is largely peaceful—an era of coconut, sugar cane, coffee, cacao and cotton plantations. The slaves are emancipated in 1836.

20th century–present

St Lucia heads gradually towards full self-government, finally granted by the West Indies Act of 1967. Independence comes in 1979, and the economy remains centred on agriculture, chiefly the export of bananas. St Lucia's farmers are hit hard by the WTO's removal of preferential tarrifs in 1997, and the government begins to develop tourism in earnest.

istockphoto.com/Geer

Cocoa is an important export: here the beans are spread out to dry.

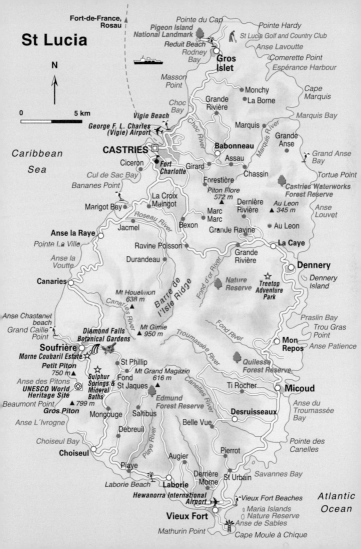

The South

In the 18th century, Maréchal de Laborie established the circular coastal road that skirts the southern corner of the island. You will probably take it to visit St Lucia's most spectacular sights, the Soufrière volcano and the majestic Pitons. If you go by car, it's wise to hire a local driver familiar with all the hair-raising bends; many also tour the southwest by way of a boat cruise, allowing you to view the spectacular coastline from the sea.

Bays and Beaches

South of Castries is **Marigot Bay**, a pleasant palm-fringed spot with several hotels and restaurants, well worth a stop off for a swim or a meal.

Further along are more attractive and quiet bays and beaches: **Anse la Raye**, a pretty collection of weatherbeaten wooden buildings that stages a lively Friday night fried-fish fest; as well as **Anse Cochon** (French for pig) and the little fishing village of **Canaries**.

Soufrière

Typically West Indian, with its graceful arcaded buildings and cut-stone **Church of the Assumption**, Soufrière town nestles just under the twin Pitons: 770 m **Gros Piton** and 743 m **Petit Piton**. The views as you descend into town are nothing short of breathtaking.

Diamond Falls Botanical Gardens and Mineral Baths

Just outside town, the main road passes by this popular visitor attraction. Its sulphurous springs were discovered by the French, and in 1784, Maréchal de Laborie, then in command of the island, sent samples to Paris. They were analyzed by Louis XVI's doctors, who pronounced the water to be beneficial. Upon this favourable news, the original baths were constructed—today, you can enjoy the same pleasurable effects. Trails lead to Diamond Falls, a pretty cascade where the mineral-laced waters have coloured the rocks in multiple shades. The surrounding gardens are planted with an array of colourful plants and flowers.

Morne Coubaril Estate

Just south of town, this 18th-century estate offers a fascinating insight into the plantation era, with guides demonstrating traditional methods for processing cocoa, coffee and sugar-cane. You can also hike through the grounds or try the adrenaline-fuelled ziplines, which offer spectacular views of Petit Piton.

Sulphur Springs

A twisting road leads from Soufrière to the Sulphur Springs, advertised as the world's only drive-in volcano. It is actually a caldera, the volcano having erupted and collapsed into itself 39,000 years ago. The road goes right into the crater, and guides walk you up to viewing platforms which overlook a rockface of steaming, boiling pools that emit a strong sulphurous odour. Until the mid-1990's, visitors could walk along the face, but this ceased when a guide slipped and fell, receiving serious burns. Efforts are being made to harness the steam energy for island use. Some rocks are coloured green by copper deposits, white by lime and chalk and yellow by sulphur.

An information centre gives plenty of background on the site and if you don't mind the smell, you can also bathe in the warm volcanic waters of a nearby stream, said to be therapeutic.

Vieux Fort to Dennery
South of Soufrière, the road passes through Choiseul and Laborie, two ramshackle but picturesque little villages. St Lucia's southern tip holds its second-largest town, **Vieux Fort**, home to Hewanorra International Airport.

Moule à Chique
Above View Fort, a lighthouse stands on Moule à Chique cape, the island's southernmost point. On a clear day the view from here is spectacular. Out to sea, you'll glimpse the island of St Vincent

and, close to the shore, the green humps of the **Maria Islands**, a protected nature reserve that's home to rare snakes and lizards. The St Lucia National Trust can arrange guided tours. The seemingly endless **Anse des Sables** beach north of the cape is buffeted by Atlantic winds. Popular with kite-surfers, it's also home to a resort hotel.

The Southeast Coast
As you travel up the southeast coast, you'll find the road somewhat easier going, not that there isn't plenty to keep a driver alert—children on their way home from school or cows, donkeys and sheep wandering on the tarmac. Headlands project into the ocean, and there are two little towns to explore, **Micoud** and **Dennery**, from where the road winds back across the island to Castries.

Inland rises **Mount Gimie**, the highest point on the island at 950 m. Dennery earned renown as a den of iniquity, and until the 1950s a part of town called Oléon (or Aux Lyons) was closed to outsiders. Townspeople made a strong (and illegal) brew known as *mal cochon*, and they were so belligerent in the defence of their privacy that even the police were reluctant to interfere.

Inland of Dennery, **Treetop Adventure Park** offers several ziplines and rainforest bike rides.

Barbados

The most easterly of the Caribbean islands, Barbados is a coral and limestone-capped isle lying in the path of cooling trade winds. Though the island measures only 34 km by 22 (21 miles by 14), its shores are blessed with almost 100 km (60 miles) of shimmering white sands. The dramatic, windswept east coast is washed by Atlantic waves, while the tranquil palm-fringed Caribbean beaches of the west coast are perfect for swimming, snorkelling and sunbathing. Barbados has 286,000 inhabitants (called Bajans), though you're rarely aware of crowds, except on a shopping day in Bridgetown, the capital.

Bridgetown
Founded in 1628, the town probably takes its name from an old Indian bridge said to have spanned the River Constitution. The colourful port, with its venerable coral-stone mansions, cool green savannahs and lively open-air markets has retained some of its British character. In 2011, historic Bridgetown and its Garrison were UNESCO-listed.

Deep Water Harbour
A little out of Bridgetown to the west, the picturesque cruise-ship harbour has its own tourist office and shopping complex. The **Chattel House Village** is a crafts centre in traditional wooden houses.

Careenage
The port of Bridgetown lies at the mouth of the River Constitution and is used mainly by yachts and sailboats. On the north side, **National Heroes Square**, formerly Trafalgar Square and renamed in 1999, marks the heart of town. The dignified bronze monument to Lord Nelson was erected in 1813, 30 years before the famous memorial in London. Bordering the square, **Broad Street** is a colourful, animated thoroughfare with old colonial buildings and shopping centres.

North of the square, you'll see the neo-Gothic **Parliament Buildings** that have housed the Barbados legislature ever since a fire destroyed most of the neighbourhood in 1860. They have been superbly restored, and an interactive **Museum Gallery** devoted to history and the national heroes is set in the west wing.

St Michael's Cathedral
The coral-stone Anglican Cathedral on St Michael's Row (1789) boasts a solid tower and attractive stained-glass.

Up the road from St Michael's, the lawns of **Queen's Park** hold a bandstand, an off-grid **Solar House**, built to show the feasibility of solar energy use, and **King's House** (1786), originally the residence of the British Commanding General and now home to an art gallery.

Belleville

To the east, this district is a residential area full of pretty Victorian houses. **Government House**, a mansion dating from the early 18th century, is home to the Governor General.

Nidhe Israel Synagogue and Museum

North of the centre, on Bruce Alley, the synagogue was originally built in 1654, but the present structure dates from 1833. It serves as a reminder that the Barbados sugar industry was founded in part by Portuguese Jews who came here via Brazil in 1627, as explored in the museum.

Mount Gay Visitor Centre

Near the cruise ship harbour, this is a temple to the island's best-known brand of rum. Guides take you through the distilling process and provide some background on the Mount Gay brand, founded in 1703. Samples are included.

Garrison Savannah

The former British military headquarters and a key part of the UNESCO site, Garrison Savannah, lies on the southern outskirts of town, its former parade ground lined with attractive colonial buildings. The old military prison houses the **Barbados Museum**, recounting the history of the island from the time of the Arawaks.

What a useful fruit is the coconut: drink and container all in one.

Rooms are focused on militaria, social history, decorative arts and African traditions and influence; there's also an interactive children's gallery.

On the west side of Garrison Savannah is the **George Washington House**, where the American President made his only foreign stay, in 1751–52. A film documents its history, and you can tour the interior and explore a museum.

South Coast

On the south coast, the beaches of **St Lawrence Gap** (or just The Gap) are famous for their riotous nightlife. Further east, **Oistins** is a busy port where fishermen unload their catch of flying fish every morning at dawn. Big fish fries are organized every Friday.

Admire the windswept and dramatic view from **Crane Beach**, in the southeast, voted one of the ten most beautiful beaches in the world despite its rough waters.

BARBADOS FLASHBACK

16th century

Barbados is discovered by Portuguese explorer Pedro a Campos in 1536. He names it los Barbudos ("the bearded ones") after the island's hoary-looking banyan trees, whose hanging roots resemble beards. But Portugal is not particularly interested in Barbados and establishes no permanent outposts there.

17th–18th centuries

An English vessel sails by and claims Barbados for Great Britain in 1625. Englishmen from the ship William and John found the island's first settlement, Jamestown (later renamed Holetown), in 1627. Large tobacco, cotton and sugar cane plantations are set up. More than 380,000 African slaves are brought in to work on the plantations.

19th century

Both black and white Barbadians enter the new century with optimism as Great Britain ends the slave trade in 1806 and abolishes slavery completely in 1834. But the island passes through hard times, with periodic massive destruction from hurricanes and a decline in the value of sugar, the principal cash crop, whose price plummets more than 50 percent in 50 years.

20th century–present

Great Britain takes steps to improve the economies of its West Indian dependencies, inaugurating an agricultural revolution on Barbados that brings new prosperity. The island begins to diversify its economy, including light industry and tourism. Barbados achieves full independence within the British Commonwealth, joining the United Nations in 1966. Tourism becomes the economy's mainstay.

The handsome Garrison Clock Tower at St Ann's Fort.

istockphoto.com/Slattery

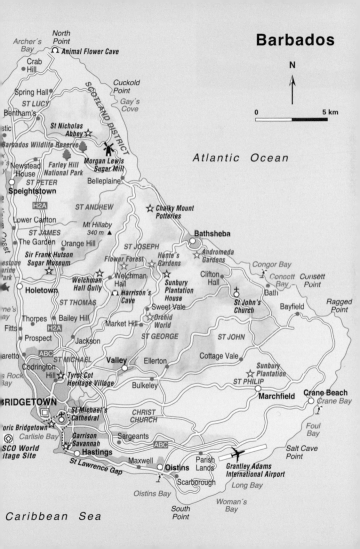

Barbados

N

0   5 km

Atlantic Ocean

Caribbean Sea

Archer's Bay
North Point
Ω Animal Flower Cave
Crab Hill
Spring Hall
ST LUCY
Bentham's
St Nicholas Abbey
Barbados Wildlife Reserve
Newstead House
Farley Hill National Park
Morgan Lewis Sugar Mill
ST PETER
Speightstown
H2A
Lower Carlton
ST ANDREW
The Garden
ST JAMES
Mt Hillaby 340 m ▲
Orange Hill
Sir Frank Hutson Sugar Museum
Flower Forest
Welchman Hall Gully
Welchman Hall
Holetown
ST THOMAS
Harrison's Cave
Thorpes
Bailey Hill
H2A
Prospect
Jackson
Market Hill
ABC
Codrington Hill
ST MICHAEL
Tyrol Cot Heritage Village
BRIDGETOWN
St Michael's Cathedral
oric Bridgetown
Carlisle Bay
SCO World itage Site
Garrison Savannah
Hastings
St Lawrence Gap
Maxwell

Cuckold Point
Gay's Cove
SCOTLAND DISTRICT
Belleplaine
Chalky Mount Potteries
Bathsheba
Andromeda Gardens
Hunte's Gardens
ST JOSEPH
Clifton Hall
Congor Bay
Consett Bay
Consett Point
Sunbury Plantation House
St John's Church
Bath
Bayfield
Ragged Point
Sweet Vale
Orchid World
ST GEORGE
ST JOHN
Valley
Ellerton
Cottage Vale
Sunbury Plantation
ST PHILIP
Bulkeley
Marchfield
Crane Beach
Crane Bay
CHRIST CHURCH
Sargeants
ABC
Foul Bay
Salt Cave Point
Parish Lands
Oistins
Scarborough
Grantley Adams International Airport
Long Bay
Oistins Bay
South Point
Woman's Bay

Sink your toes into the warm Caribbean sand.

Huber/Mackie

Atlantic Coast

The east coast shows off Barbados' wild side. Lashed by Atlantic waves , it is a popular place to go surfing, with afficionados heading to top spots such as the Soup Bowl at Bathsheba.

Perched 250 m above sea level, **St John's Church** offers lovely views of lush countryside. The present structure dates back to 1836, and the cemetery, older still, contains the green-painted grave of Ferdinando Paleologus, possibly a descendant of the Byzantine emperors.

Bathsheba

The colourful wooden houses of this fishing village cling gallantly to the chalky cliffs high above the raging waters that surfers adore. Up on the heights, the **Andromeda Gardens** are a must on any east coast tour. This botanical garden contains dozens of varieties of indigenous flowers and trees. Among them is the shaggy banyan tree that inspired the name "Barbados".

Platinum Coast

The west coast takes its name from the brilliant white of its sandy beaches. Many luxury hotels and big private mansions are situated along this "Millionaire's Row". Nevertheless, between the resort developments and imposing estates, you can still see some pretty wooden houses built in traditional Barbadian style.

Holetown

A monument here commemorates the first landing of a British ship on Barbados in 1625. The Anglican **St James's Church** was founded three years later and rebuilt in 1874; it preserves a bell and font from the 17th century.

The nearby **Folkestone Marine Reserve** is popular with snorkellers and divers; boat cruises also offer the chance to snorkel with turtles. Neighbouring **Payne's Bay** is a dazzling white-sand beach.

Speightstown

This was once the sugar capital of the northwest area. It was known as "Little Bristol", since the Speight family made most of their trade with the English port. Speightstown has remained typically West Indian, with small, pastel wooden houses and shops and its old church.

The **Arlington House Museum** looks into local history. A luxury marina has been built at Port Charles.

The North

At the northern tip of the island is **Animal Flower Cave**, where a guide will lead you down steep steps to a cavern by the sea, named for an exquisite sea anemone. The swimming is lovely and there's a restaurant and bar.

On the return journey, stop at **St Nicholas Abbey**, a superb plantation house. One of the oldest in the Caribbean, it was built around 1650 in Jacobean style with Dutch gables. Its old steam mill has been restored. A short distance east stands the **Morgan Lewis Sugar Mill**, dating from 1727 and carefully restored.

Going north, you will come to **Farley Hill National Park**, named for its ruined plantation house and offering walking trails and beautiful views of the Atlantic coast. Opposite, the small **Barbados Wildlife Reserve** displays iguanas, caymans, birds and green monkeys, some of them in the wild of the mahogany forest.

The Interior

At **Welchman Hall Gully**, you can also see green monkeys in the mornings. This deep and wide ravine, dotted with caves, was planted with citrus and spices and has developed into a precipitous botanical garden. Nearby, a little tourist tram visits **Harrison's Cave**, with its impressive stalagmites and stalactites.

Toward the coast, **Sunbury Plantation House** dates from 1660, and its interior has been furnished in period style, with plenty of locally made mahogany furniture. The cellars house a collection of antique horse-drawn carriages.

In the same region, the **Flower Forest** of the Richmond Plantation has superb displays of pink and red bougainvillea, set out in rows. The more poetic **Hunte's Gardens**, in another ravine, are planted with large trees, flowers and orchids—and wicker chairs.

Garden-lovers will also love **Orchid World**, off the road from Bathsheba to Bridgetown. It has more than 20,000 orchids.

To the southwest, on Codrington Hill, **Tyrol Cot Heritage Village** is a museum set in the former home of Sir Grantley Adams (1898–1971), first Premier of Barbados.

St Vincent and the Grenadines

St Vincent surges from the sea like a comet, capped by a simmering volcano and trailing a tail of islets in its wake—the glistening Grenadines. Constant and intense volcanic activity through the ages has endowed St Vincent with a fringe of shiny black-sand beaches, notably on the Atlantic side. Yet the spectacular coast can melt into lush terraced hills a few miles inland, and in the south the beaches are golden coral. La Soufrière, an active volcano, dominates the island's entire northern end. Nature has been kind to St Vincent's 100,000 inhabitants. Bananas, coconuts, cocoa and yams all flourish on the "Breadfruit Island"—it was the first in the Caribbean to be planted with the fruit brought from the South Pacific by the legendary Captain Bligh.

Kingstown
St Vincent's attractive capital lies on a sheltered bay in the southwest. Its streets are lined with pretty stone arcades, many of them left over from French colonial times.

Harbour and Markets
Surrounded by high green hills, the harbour is always alive with schooners and fishing boats, and with ferries arriving and departing for the Grenadine islands. On the eastern edge of the harbour, cruise ships anchor at a special quay with shops, restaurants, a tourist office and other facilities.

To the west along Bay Street (next to the main bus terminal) is the big covered **fish market**. Just inland, Kingstown's **food market** ranks among the best in the Caribbean, and is especially busy at weekends.

Churches
In Grenville Street, towards the other end of town, you'll see an ecumenical trio. **St George's Anglican Cathedral** has a stained-glass window that was designed for St Paul's in London; Queen Victoria refused it because the angel is dressed in red.

The **Methodist Church** dates from 1841 and **St Mary's Roman Catholic Church** from 1823. This last, a fanciful pot-pourri of Romanesque, Gothic and Renaissance styles, would delight any storybook illustrator. There are towers, crosses and fretwork, added in the 1930s when it was restored by monks.

Botanic Gardens
In a hilly setting just behind the Governor's Residence, the Botanic Gardens were founded in 1765, and are one of the oldest in the Western Hemisphere. Delightfully landscaped, they feature ponds and shady paths.

ST VINCENT AND THE GRENADINES FLASHBACK

15th–17th centuries

Columbus discovers St Vincent in 1498. The Carib Indians fiercely resist British and French attempts to colonize the island. The Grenadines come under a Norman feudal lord, Jacques Diel du Parquet. Escaped and ship-wrecked African slaves begin intermarrying with the natives towards the end of the 17th century, creating a new race, the Black Caribs.

18th century

St Vincent passes back and forth between the British and French. In 1795, the islanders side with the French against the British colonizers in the Brigands' War, but the British overcome the opposition and banish over 5,000 troublemakers from Bequia (mostly Carib Indians) to Honduras. This time Britannia rules for nearly two centuries.

19th century–present

Britain outlaws slave-trading throughout its colonies in 1807 and slavery itself in 1833. Indentured labourers are brought in a few years later from Portugal and India to work the cane fields. Future King George V and his brother Prince Alfred visit the Grenadines in 1880. St Vincent and Grenada both become British Associate States in the 1960s but then gain independence in the 1970s. The Grenadines are split up between Grenada and St Vincent, with the dividing line on the northern extremity of Carriacou. Yachtsmen, and then tourists, discover the Grenadines. In 2009 the people vote to remain within the Commonwealth.

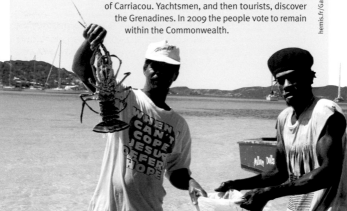

hemis.fr/Gardel

Fort Charlotte

Just west of Kingstown, this sturdy fort stands 194 m above the sea, offering a panoramic view of the capital, harbour and the closest Grenadines. It was built by the British as a defence against the French and was named after the wife of King George III.

You can see the lookout point and three of the cannon still in place, turned towards the interior to fend off Carib attacks.

The inmates of the **Women's Prison**, a short distance downhill, look out on one of the loveliest views in the world.

Caribbean Coast

From Kingstown, drive north-west via the Leeward Highway, the narrow road that twists its way along the coast. As you travel northwards, folds in the coastline reveal one stunning sea view after another, from black-sand beaches to picturesque vil-

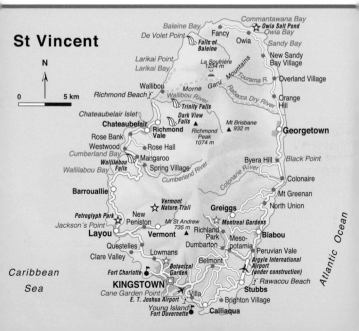

St Vincent

N

0 5 km

Baleine Bay
De Volet Point
Commantawana Bay
Owia Salt Pond
Fancy
Owia Bay
Owia
Sandy Bay
Falls of Baleine
New Sandy Bay Village
Larikai Point
Larikai Bay
La Soufrière 1234 m
Garu
Mountains
Tourama R.
Overland Village
Wallibou
Morne
Wallibou River
Trinity Falls
Rebecca Dry River
Orange Hill
Richmond Beach
Chateaubelair Islet
Dark View Falls
Mt Brisbane ▲ 932 m
Georgetown
Chateaubelair
Richmond Vale
Richmond Peak 1074 m
Rose Bank
Westwood
Rose Hall
Cumberland Bay
Mangaroo
Byera Hill
Black Point
Wallilbou Falls
Spring Village
Cumberland River
Colonarie River
Colonaire
Wallilabou Bay
Barrouallie
Mt Greenan
North Union
Vermont Nature Trail
Greiggs
Montreal Gardens
Petroglyph Park
New Peniston
Mt St Andrew 735 m
Jackson's Point
Richland Park
Biabou
Layou
Vermont
Meso-potamia
Questelles
Lowmans
Dumbarton
Peruvian Vale
Clare Valley
Belmont
Argyle International Airport (under construction)
Fort Charlotte
Botanical Garden
Rawacou Beach
KINGSTOWN
Stubbs
Cane Garden Point
Villa
E. T. Joshua Airport
Brighton Village
Young Island
Fort Duvernette
Calliaqua

Caribbean Sea

Atlantic Ocean

lages framed by palm groves. At the end of Buccament Valley, the **Vermont Nature Trails** loop into the rainforest and pass through the **St Vincent Parrot Reserve**, home to the island's endemic species.

Layou Petroglyph Park

Just before the small fishing village of Layou Bay, set in a park overlooking the ocean and the Buccament Bay resort, stop to admire the Indian petroglyphs, stone carvings estimated to be at least 1,400 years old. A short trail leads up to the smooth rock face, carved with several designs. You can take in the views from the gazebo, and there's also a natural pool if you fancy a dip. Others can be seen in the school grounds at **Barrouallie**. This village, 5 km (3 miles) further along the road, is a centre of traditional pilot-whale fishing.

Beaches and Waterfalls

The splendid, wild **Walillabou Bay** has been basking in the fame it acquired when scenes from the second *Pirates of the Caribbean* were filmed there. The stage set remains in place, getting ever more weatherbeaten each year. Nearby, **Walillabou Falls** is a pretty little swimming spot.

Some 48 km (30 miles) from Kingstown, the tarmac comes to an end near **Richmond Beach**, ideal for a picnic or swim. A driveable track leads to **Dark View Falls**, with two waterfalls and a nice pool for swimming. There are no roads serving the northwest part of the island, so the only way to reach the **Falls of Baleine** is by boat.

The South

Southeast along the coast, past the Kingstown airport, you reach the main resort area of St Vincent, with a few hotels and some golden-sand beaches.

Young Island

This private island has been developed as a luxury resort hotel. For a small fee, you'll be permitted to use the pool or the small beach. **Fort Duvernette**, on an adjacent islet, is reputed to have figured in battles with the Caribs.

Mesopotamia

The Vigie Highway climbs the lower slopes of Mt St Andrew to the **Belmont Lookout**, commanding a spectacular view over the Mesopotamia Valley. Richly cultivated fields clad the neatly terraced hillsides interspersed with a score of pretty villages. A winding branch road goes to **Montreal Gardens**, a tranquil and beautifully landscaped retreat networked with pathways. The tree ferns and anthurium garden are particularly impressive.

istockphoto.com/Alia

istockphoto.com/Tilghman

Banana blossom: purple bracts protecting the male flowers. | An adolescent green sea turtle.

Atlantic Coast

The Windward Highway parallels the shimmering volcanic black-sand beaches of the east coast. Bathing is not advised because of the strong undertow, but you can swim in the pools of **Rawacou Beach**, near the new **Argyle International Airport** at Mount Pleasant, due to open in 2016.

From here you drive through more rugged Atlantic scenery. Enjoy the superb beach at **Black Point**; at its southern end is a tunnel dug by slaves, around 1815, to facilitate loading sugar onto boats for export. The banana capital of **Georgetown** has seen better days. Beyond it, the road passes through a huge coconut plantation as well as the last villages inhabited by Black Caribs: **Sandy Bay**, **Owia** and **Fancy**, at the northern tip of the island. The picturesque **Owia Salt Pond** offers swimming in rocky pools.

La Soufrière

Just outside Georgetown, a narrow winding road goes through fruit plantations towards the volcano. From its end there's a further 2-hour hike through tangled bamboo and rainforest to reach the crater, at 1,235 m. Nearing the top, the forest gives way to arborescent plants then to a windswept moor.

La Soufrière's chief, most recent eruption occurred between March and May 1902, a few days before that of Martinique's Mont Pelée, in which 1,600 people lost their lives. Following the 1902 eruption, a beautiful lake formed in La Soufrière's huge crater, which briefly featured a lava-dome island before a minor eruption in 1979 saw the lake disappear, replaced with the mass of whitish-grey hot ash that you see today. Trekking down the west side of the volcano with a guide takes about 3 hours.

The Grenadines

So remote are these islands that opinions differ as to just how many there are. Counting all the islets and rocky outcrops, some only a few yards across, they total around 600, of which some 125 constitute the core of the Grenadines. The northern two-thirds of the island chain are administered by St Vincent. Some are rich in vegetation, with sheltered harbours and coves offering sailing and sunbathing. Others are rocky and uninhabited, unvisited due to sheer, breathtaking cliffs.

Bequia

Just 18 sq km (7 sq miles) in area, Bequia lies 15 km (9 miles) from St Vincent. Visitors come by plane or take the ferry to **Port Elizabeth** in Admiralty Bay. The tourist office near the dock will help you fix island tours and hire cars and drivers by the day.

The quaint waterfront and the **Belmont Walkway** are lined with bars, restaurants and shops. On the beach, fishermen mend their nets and hand-build their boats, maintaining age-old traditions and Bequia's most important industry. In town, two renowned workshops turn out scale models of sailing ships.

Bequia's main sights can be covered in half a day, starting with **Bequia Maritime Museum**, on

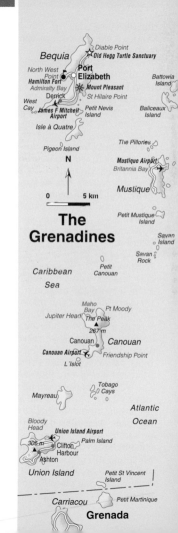

the western side of the bay. Above it, the ruins of **Hamilton Fort** afford fine coastal views. The whaling museum at **Friendship Bay** is quite small, but the port is still used by some of the island families for harpoon fishing, a few days a year. From **Mount Pleasant** you get a good view of the island, and in the northeast, the **Old Hegg Turtle Sanctuary** gives you the chance to see green turtles.

End your visit with a swim at the extraordinary **Princess Margaret Beach** near Port Elizabeth, noted for its coral reef and excellent snorkelling. The sands at the adjacent **Lower Bay** are just as alluring.

Mustique

The name comes from the French word for mosquito, but this shouldn't put you off. After all, the green and hilly island with its impressive and exclusive colony of villas has attracted some of the world's richest and most famous people. Princess Margaret was given a plot of land as a wedding present; she adored staying here, but when she gave her holiday home, Jolies Eaux, to her son Viscount Linley he promptly sold it, much to her chagrin. For all its publicity, Mustique still remains secluded, and looks more like a desert isle than a gathering place for the jet set.

Most of the accommodation on the island is privately owned, but you can stay in villas managed by the Mustique Company, or book in at the sprinkling of hotels, which include the lavish **Cotton House**. Unless you rent one of the villas or are the guest of someone who owns one, you are unlikely to go further than the turquoise waters of **Britannia Bay**, a famous yachtsmen's and sailors' haunt that is home to the legendary **Basil's Bar** — an essential stop off for a cocktail or a meal overlooking the water.

Canouan

Canouan claims some of the best beaches in the Caribbean. Long hot ribbons of powdery white sand blend with warm clear water and coral. The 2,000 inhabitants are mostly farmers and fishermen. The island has been developed as a discreet resort, with a large hotel, golf course and a few guest houses.

Tobago Cays Marine Park

The cays are five uninhabited islets surrounded by spectacular coral reefs. This protected reserve is the perfect paradise for escapists. There is sailing, snorkelling, swimming and picnicking in seclusion — a rare tropical Eden, normally reached by chartered yacht or on a day cruise from the surrounding islands.

Mayreau

Tiny Mayreau has just a sprinkling of roads and a tiny local population. On the highest hill, the single village snuggles round a delightful Catholic church, built by a French family in the early 1800s and still a Sunday gathering place for the locals.

Saltwhistle Bay harbours the island's only hotel resort. The beach here is one of the most sheltered in the Grenadines, perfect for children.

Union

Here you're almost back to civilization! There's an airport, a bank and even a small hospital. But don't worry, as elsewhere in the Grenadines, the main charm is sheer escapism. The island's silhouette is distinctive, with the impressive Mount Parnassus, "the Pinnacle", soaring from the sea. Clifton Harbour, the main town, is small but commercial.

Palm

Privately owned, this flat, 55-ha (54-acre) island was named for the coconut palms lining its white-sand beaches. A resort-hotel, it offers every kind of water sport and tennis. Life here is casual but chic.

Petit St Vincent

The southernmost St Vincent Grenadine, Petit St Vincent (PSV) is more hilly than its neighbour Palm, and its sole development is its lavish, up-market resort hotel.

Underwater Wonderland. A host of exotic creatures inhabit the watery depths of the Caribbean. Apart from beautiful flower-like sea anemones, common sights include elkhorn, finger and brain coral, which look exactly as their names imply. In addition, you may see fire and pillar coral, as well as sea fans. Take care not to step on the razor-sharp coral, and refrain from touching their fragile formations. Slow to grow and easily damaged, coral reefs are formed by tiny animals called polyps which live in surface cavities and feed on plankton.

Fish are not all shy about parading their gorgeous colours past snorkellers and divers. Look for the bright-blue-and-yellow Queen Angelfish, the orange-and-blue Honeytail Damselfish and striking Queen Triggerfish. The blue Ocean Surgeon has a neat "incision" marked in black on its gill, and the Sergeant-Major sports pretty blue, yellow and black stripes.

Corbis/Westmorland

Grenada

One of the most southerly of the Caribbean chain, Grenada is said to be the most beautiful island of the Antilles. Spice has always been a way of life here. But in 2004 Hurricane Ivan destroyed many of the plantations, drastically reducing Grenada's contribution to world production of nutmeg, as well as cinnamon, cloves, pepper, bay leaves, saffron and mace. The island has recovered quickly, however, and the vibrant lifestyle of Grenada's 110,000 inhabitants matches the luxuriance of its natural assets. Dense carpets of tropical rainforest drape the volcanic mountains in a tangle of coconut palms, lianas and flowering shrubs. Waterfalls cascade down the hillsides. To the north lie the tiny Grenadines, of which Carriacou, Petit-Martinique and several islets belong to Grenada.

St George's

Built on hills surrounding one of Caribbean's most picturesque harbours, the island capital's English Georgian and French provincial houses preserve the flavour of its colonial past.

The Carenage

Along the Carenage, the curving waterfront of the inner harbour, attractive 18th-century warehouses line the north side of the quay. The rounded shape of the harbour is due to its origins as an ancient submerged crater. High on a hill overlooking the harbour stands **Fort George**, erected by the French in 1705. It was here that the radical Prime Minister Maurice Bishop and thirteen of his ministers were executed in 1984—a plaque marks the spot. Five English cannon are lined up over the cruise ships.

Markets

Sendall Tunnel leads from the Carenage to the Esplanade and its shopping centre that draws cruise ship passengers. One street further, **Market Square** is the site of a typical West Indian open-air market overflowing with local spices, fruit, vegetables and crafts. It's at its busiest on Saturdays but closes on Sunday. The **fish market** is a short stroll to the north.

National Museum

On Young Street, in an old French barracks, the museum shows its age but is still quite appealing. It displays all kinds of objects ranging from Pre-Columbian remains to the bathtub of Empress Josephine.

Fort Frederick

Up on Richmond Hill, the fort is a splendid lookout point. Construction was begun by the French in 1779, but it was the British who finished it off in 1783.

GRENADA FLASHBACK

Pre-Columbian era

By AD 300, the Arawak Indians from South America have settled throughout the Caribbean. They are driven out by the warlike Caribs, also from South America.

15th–17th centuries

In 1498, Columbus discovers Grenada on his third voyage. It is inhabited by warlike Caribs, who drive out the Arawaks, an Indian tribe that settled throughout the Caribbean before ad 300. Columbus calls the island Concepción, but later Spanish sailors rename it after their native Granada. Early attempts by both British and French to subdue the Caribs fail, and it is not until 1650 that the French establish a foothold. They carry out a campaign of extermination against the Caribs. When defeat is certain, the last small group of Indians jump to their deaths from a northern cliff. Slaves are brought in to work the sugar plantations.

18th century

The British oust the French from Grenada in 1762 but are driven out in 1779. France holds the island for four years, until the Treaty of Versailles (1783) awards it to Britain. In 1795, a slave uprising provokes bloody reprisals.

19th century

Slavery is abolished in all British colonies in 1834. Contract workers from India begin arriving to replace slave labour on the Caribbean plantations. In 1843, nutmeg is introduced to Grenada from the Dutch East Indies and soon takes over from sugar as the island's principal export. Grenada is formally declared a Crown Colony of Britain in 1877.

20th century–present

An elected legislature is created in 1924 and the island is made a British Associated State in 1967. Grenada achieves full independence in 1974 but remains within the British Commonwealth. A coup d'état in the spring of 1979 deposes Prime Minister Sir Eric Gairy and installs Maurice Bishop at the head of a People's Revolutionary Government. In the autumn of 1983, Maurice Bishop is killed during an attempted takeover by the extremist elements of his own party. Cuban involvement prompts a military invasion by the United States; the US forces leave in 1985. Today the economy is based on agriculture and tourism.

Carriacou

Gun Point
Anse la Roche
Windward
Watering Bay
Petit Carenage Bay
Petit St Vincent Island
Petit Martinique Island

Diamond Island
Ronde Island
Ta

Hillsborough Bay
Mabouya Island
Sandy Island
Jack Iron Point
L'Esterre
Hospital Hill
Hillsborough
Tarleton Point
Grand Bay

Caille Island

Tyrrel Bay
Belmont
Kendeace Point
Manchineel Bay
Southwest Point
Saline Island
Frigate Island
Large Island

London Bridge Island

David Point
Duquesne Bay
Sauteurs
Levera National Park
Levera Pond
Sugar Loaf
Green Island
Sandy Island
Bathway Beach
Grenada Bay

Nonpareil
St Mark Bay
Union
Chantimelle
R. Sallee

Victoria

Mt St Catherine
840 m

Belmont Estate
Peggy's Whim
Lake Antoine
River Antoine Distillery
Tivoli
La Poterie

Moya
Pearls Rock

Gouyave
Gouyave Bay

Caribbean Sea

Carriacou, Petit Martinique
Palmiste Point
Dougaldston Estate
Little River
Simon River
Bylands
Paradise
Great River Bay
Telescope Point

Grand Roy
Concord
Concord Falls
Halifax Harbour

Grand Etang National Park
Annandale Falls
Granton
Willis
Vendome
Ravine
Mardigras
Perdmontemps
Great River
Grand Etang Road
Birch Grove
Seven Falls
Mount Lebanon
715 m
Mount Sinai
703 m
St Francis R.
Munich
Mount Carmel Waterfalls
Marquis
Grenville Bay
Grenville
Marquis Island
Grea Bacolet Point

Moliniere Point
Underwater Sculpture Park
Grand Mal Bay

Fort George
ST GEORGE'S
Fort Frederick
Pomme Rose
Bacolet
Corinth
St David's
La Tante Bay
Requin Bay

Atlantic Ocean

N

Grand Anse Bay
Grand Anse
Calliste
Ruth Howard
Galivigny
La Sagesse Bay
St David's Point
Westerhall Point

Morne Rouge Bay
Point Salines
Maurice Bishop International Airport
Lance aux Epines
Glover Island
Prickly Point
Calivigny Island

0   5

Grenada

The South

Take a water taxi from the Carenage or drive to Grenada's most beautiful beach, **Grand Anse Bay**, with countless hotels. Its shimmering white sand stretches for more than 3 km (2 miles). Further down the coast is a succession of lovely stretches of sand, starting with **Morne Rouge Bay** (BBC Beach), surrounded by arid hills and offering excellent diving.

Around the headland past the **Maurice Bishop International Airport**, **L'Anse aux Epines** holds a sprinkling of resort hotels and restaurants along the golden-sand beach.

West Coast

The scenic route north along the western coast offers bays and headlands of uncommon beauty interspersed with pretty fishing villages. You'll see wooden huts, brightly painted boats and long seine nets hanging out to dry.

Underwater Sculpture Park,

Just outside St George's, **Moliniere Bay** is home to one of the Caribbean's most unusual marine attractions: around 80 eerie figures in various poses lie right on the seabed. Most are by British artist Jason de Cairies Taylor and are becoming slowly encrusted with coral and marine life, and with the surrounding reefs this is an incredible spot to go snorkelling.

Gouyave

On the main street of Grenada's fishing capital, Gouyave, the **Nutmeg Processing Co-Operative** is an atmospheric factory where this fragrant spice is sorted and dried in preparation for shipping all over the world. You can learn more about local spices and processing methods just outside town at the **Dougaldston Estate**.

Northern Tip

Near the village of Sauteurs is **Morne des Sauteurs** (Leaper's Hill), the rocks from which the last of the Carib Indians plummeted to death in 1650 rather than surrender to the French.

To the east lies **Levera National Park**, with a delightfully wild beach overlooked by the conical Sugar Loaf island. Sea turtles nest on the sand and there's a pond surrounded by mangroves, harbouring a large variety of birds.

East Coast

The white sands of **Bathway Beach** are a great place to swim, with a wall of reef protecting the water from the Atlantic waves. Past here, take a turnoff to **Lake Antoine**, a former volcanic crater that's home to a variety of birdlife. Just beyond is the extraordinary **River Antoine Distillery**, whose production methods have barely changed since 1785; tastings are available.

Inland, you can tour the operations at the **Belmont Estate**, an active cocoa plantation with a good restaurant.

Grenville, Grenada's third-largest town seems more like a casual village, with a lively market. Just south, the cool cascades of **Mount Carmel Waterfall** are a short walk from the road.

Grand-Etang Road
Connecting St George and Grenville, the hairpin turns of Grand-Etang Road take you through tropical rainforests and gorges of exceptional beauty. The road passes right through **Grand Etang National Park**, with its 12-ha (30-acre) crater lake, often shrouded in mist. From the visitor centre above the lake, several marked trails head into the forest—keep your eyes open for the wild monkeys living here.

Towards St George, a winding branch road takes you to the popular **Annandale Falls**.

Carriacou
An island of green hills and sandy beaches, Carriacou is the largest of the Grenadines and lies 37 km (23 miles) northeast of Grenada. The 6,000-strong population has mixed origins: French, Scottish and African. Traditional culture has been preserved, with "Big Drum Dances" still held around Easter time.

Hillsborough and Tyrrel Bay
In the capital (population 800), seek out the interesting **Carriacou Historical Society Museum** on Paterson Street, which displays exhibits from Amerindian settlements and examines the local ship-building techniques originally introduced by a Glaswegian immigrant.

At **Tyrrel Bay** you can watch boatbuilders at work, using white cedar from Grenada to make sturdy schooners without the use of power tools. To the northeast of Hillsborough, climb **Hospital Hill** for the views, and swim at **Paradise Beach**. From there water taxis go to **Sandy Island**, another paradise.

Other Sights
On the northwest coast, the fine, isolated beach of **Anse La Roche** is best reached by water taxi. There are no facilities, so take a picnic. You can walk from here to **Gun Point**, the island's northern tip, and **Petit Carenage Bay** with coral sand. A little further down the east coast, **Windward** was settled mainly by Scotsmen.

Petit Martinique
The Osprey ferry runs twice a week from Hillsborough to this dot of an island 5 km (3 miles) to the northeast. The 900 inhabitants live mainly from fishing. There are a couple of guesthouses, one church and one road.

THE HARD FACTS

Communications. There are call centres at most cruise ship ports. Country codes are: St Kitts and Nevis (869); Dominica (767); St Lucia (758); Barbados (246); St Vincent and the Grenadines (764); Grenada (473). To call the UK, dial 011 44, then the local code and your number. Roaming costs for mobile phones can be high, but you can purchase a local SIM card cheaply and easily, and top up credit as you need it. Most cruise ports have Internet cafés, and the majority of hotels and guesthouses offer Internet too. A growing number of cafes and restaurants (and some cruise ports) also offer wi-f.

Driving. Traffic drives on the left. Renting a car is the most flexible way to get round the islands. For the smaller isles, another option is to rent a motorcycle or scooter. Roads are often narrow and winding so drive carefully and defensively, and always respect the speed limits.

Emergencies. St Kitts and Nevis: police and ambulance 911, fire 333; Dominica: 999 for all services; St Lucia: 911 for all services; Barbados: police 211, fire 311, ambulance 511; St Vincent and the Grenadines: 999/911 for all services; Grenada: 911.

Languages. English is the official language in all the islands, but French Creole patois is also spoken in St Lucia.

Money. The East Caribbean dollar (EC$ or XCD), divided into 100 cents, is used on St Kitts and Nevis, Dominica, St Lucia, St Vincent and the Grenadines and Grenada. Coins from 1 ¢ to EC$1; banknotes from EC$5 to EC$100. Barbados uses the Barbados dollar (B$); coins are from 1 ¢ to B$1; banknotes from B$2 to B$100. Credit cards are widely accepted, and there are banks and ATMs in all larger towns.

Transport. Most islands have a bus service, sometimes government-run, sometimes just private individuals driving minibuses along set routes. Regular taxis are widely available but not metered, so always agree on a fare before you set off.

Water. Tap water on all the islands is chlorinated and safe to drink, but bottled mineral water is widely available.

During Trinidad's Carnival, thousands of revellers dance in the streets.

TRINIDAD AND TOBAGO

Take a Caribbean island endowed with rich natural resources and lush scenery, people it with a variety of nationalities and faiths, add the calypso and the steel-band sound, and there you have a thumbnail sketch of Trinidad. Together with its small neighbour Tobago, much the opposite in atmosphere and character, it forms the Republic of Trinidad and Tobago, with Port of Spain as its capital.

Trinidad

Originally part of South America, Trinidad and Tobago became separate islands following shifts of the Caribbean tectonic plates some 10,000 years ago. Today, Trinidad lies just 11 km (7 miles) north of Venezuela, and shares its rock formations, flora and fauna with that of the mainland. Trinidad is just 80 km (50 miles) long by 56 km (35 miles) wide and has 1.3 million inhabitants.

Port of Spain

Verdant hills surround the capital, and the people live in everything from modest wooden homes to imposing colonial mansions. The architecture embraces a variety of styles from neo-Gothic to glossy contemporary, and the restaurants vary from sushi to local *roti* stands. Port of Spain is dotted with parks of all shapes and sizes, which provide some valuable breathing space in this busy and often traffic-choked city.

Frederick Street

A short walk from the small cruise terminal, this shop-lined main thoroughfare runs north to Queen's Park Savannah. Street vendors congregate at the lower end on **Independence Square**, laid out by the Spanish as a military parade ground. Its pedestrianized central section, named **Brian Lara Promenade** in honour of Trinidad's famous cricketer, serves as an assembly point for participants in carnival parades. The Catholic **Cathedral of the Immaculate Conception** is a simple bluestone structure of 1832, with two bell towers and a vaulted interior.

TRINIDAD AND TOBAGO FLASHBACK

15th–16th centuries
Columbus sights Trinidad on his third voyage in 1498. It is inhabited by Caribs. Spain founds a colony in 1532 but uses it mainly as a base from which to search for the gold of El Dorado. In 1598 Sir Walter Raleigh burns down the newly founded Spanish town of San José and discovers Pitch Lake, using its tar to caulk his ships.

17th–18th centuries
The English attempt to settle Tobago, but disease and Carib raids decimate the inhabitants. The Dutch invade in 1658, then English privateers take over (1666), followed the next year by the French, and so on, changing hands dozens of times. African slaves are imported to work in the plantations on both islands. Tobago is declared neutral territory in 1748, but Anglo-French rivalry intensifies. Around 1770, when the first slave uprising occurs, there are 3,000 African inhabitants and only 200 whites. From 1781 the French hold sway, but the British regain control in 1793. In 1783, a Spanish royal proclamation calls upon Catholics of all nationalities to settle on Trinidad. The British capture Trinidad in 1797, but Spain does not concede ownership until 1802.

19th century
Tobago changes hands between Britain and France until 1814, when the British are back to stay. Slavery is abolished in 1833 and thousands of indentured labourers from India and the Far East are recruited to replace the slave workforce. Sugar, cotton and rum production flourish. Tobago becomes a Crown Colony in 1877, but prosperity ends abruptly in 1884 with the collapse of the sugar market. Five years later Tobago is joined to Trinidad.

20th century–present
Oil is discovered on Trinidad. During World War II the US builds bases on Trinidad to protect the Caribbean. The two islands gain independence in 1962. In 1976 Trinidad and Tobago becomes a republic, remaining within the Commonwealth, with a president as Head of State. Tobago has a separate House of Assembly. Oil plays a dominant role in the economy and tourism begins to develop, particularly in Tobago.

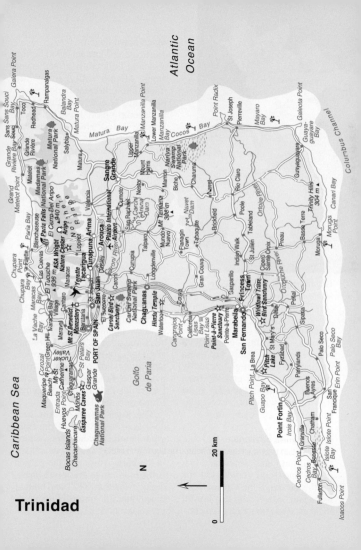

Tiny frangipani flowers fill the air with their fragrance.

Woodford Square

Overlooking this tree-shaded square are the stately **Red House** parliament building (currently under restoration) and the neo-Gothic Anglican **Cathedral of the Holy Trinity**, with its carved mahogany altar and choir stalls.

Queen's Park Savannah

This vast expanse of greenery has football and cricket pitches, fish ponds and food stands. On the south side stands the **National Museum and Art Gallery**, with displays of local art and industrial artefacts.

Magnificent Seven

North along Maraval Road lies an amazing collection of old mansions, though sadly, many are dilapidated. **Roomor** is decorated in a frothy Creole style that belies its description of "French Second Empire". Moorish-style **White Hall** has served as the Prime Minister's office. **Stollmeyer's Castle** (Killarney) belonged to a an entrepreneur who was the first to use pitch from Pitch Lake as a road surface and who made his fortune by shipping asphalt to Europe. This turreted, crenellated stone affair in Scottish baronial style has long been under repair.

Emperor Valley Zoo

On the northern side of the Savannah, the recently refurbished zoo contains a lion, White Bengal tigers (which had cubs in 2015), giraffes, jaguars, numerous monkeys and apes as well as cayman alligators, otters, snakes, ocelots and many colourful birds from macaws to toucans. It was named for Trinidad's black-and-turquoise Emperor butterflies.

The **Royal Botanic Gardens** next door boast everything from frangipani to the raw beef tree, which seems to bleed when a cut is made in the bark. Adjoining the garden is the elabourate **President's House**, dating from the 1870's and built of bluestone; it's currently undergoing restoration.

Fort George

You'll want to admire the view of town from Fort George, on the outskirts. The small house at the top of the fort overlooks the Paria Bay. On a clear day you can see all the way to Venezuela from this 334-m vantage point.

Chaguaramas

Trinidad's western peninsula has a waterside boardwalk and leisure activities at **Williams Bay**, while **Tucker Valley** offers hiking, ziplining and **Macqueripe beach**. Head out to the **Bocas islands** to swim and explore **Gasparee Caves**.

Carnival and Calypso. French settlers first brought the custom of carnival to the Caribbean; in Trinidad it has developed into a national art form, and is the biggest event of the year. The Spaniards added their own inspiration, and, after emancipation in 1834, freed slaves brought new rhythms and music, imaginative instruments made from bamboo, gourds, bottles and pans. Today, tension and excitement build up in the weeks preceding carnival in Port of Spain as everyone prepares for the big event, which is limited to just two days, from 4 a.m. Monday to midnight on Shrove Tuesday. The festivities open with the early-hours Jou vert, a raucous street parade where participants get coated in mud, body paint and even cocoa. By Monday morning, they have been replaced by costume bands, with thousands of masqueraders dancing through the streets to the soca music blasted from huge trucks. Tuesday sees Carnival bands displaying all their finery in a riot of colour and pageantry; helped along by libations of rum, the action is especially frenetic at the Queen's Park Savannah stage.

The steel band, a musical way of life all over the Caribbean, originated in Trinidad in 1937, when a group marched into Port of Spain during a carnival parade banging out a melody on old oil drums. The sound soon caught on, with a "pan tuner" today commanding great respect. The metal is tempered by heat, then hammered, the tuner making indentations that make different sounds when struck with mallets. The Trinis also take credit for inventing the calypso, said to have its origins in West Africa. The music combines African rhythms with French, Spanish and Indian elements, a sound-picture of this unique island heritage, which you'll also notice in Trinidad and Tobago's architecture, its food and its people.

The scarlet ibis: a sacred bird and a national symbol.

Island Sights

Trinidad holds a wealth of natural attractions.

Caroni Swamp

About 11 km (7 miles) southeast of Port of Spain, take a boat tour through the mangroves to see flocks of scarlet ibis, their flame-coloured feathers lighting up the greenery as they fly in to roost.

West Coast

Midway down the west coast, the **Point-a-Pierre Wildfowl Trust** sits in the middle of an oil refinery. Nearby at Waterloo, the **Temple in the Sea** Hindu shrine is lapped by ocean waters. Nearby, the **Indian Caribbean Museum** documents the lives of Trinidad's indentured workers, and the Hindu **Hanuman Murti** statue demonstrates their faith. Southwest at La Brea, the wrinkled black expanse of the **Pitch Lake** is the world's largest natural deposit of pitch.

The Northern Range

Cutting deep into the Northern Range Mountains, **Maracas–St Joseph Valley** offers the mighty **Maracas Waterfall** and a close encounter with hummingbirds at **Yerette**, where sugar-feeders and a flowered garden attract hundreds of dazzling little specimens.

In the neighbouring valley, a museum in the former cocoa plantation of **Lopinot** is set in beautiful tree-shaded gardens.

Asa Wright Nature Centre

High up in the Northern Range hills, this is a great spot to see some of the colourful birds which inhabit Trinidad's forests, which are attracted to the bird feeders at the centre's balcony. You can also tour the grounds to catch a glimpse of the rare cave-dwelling oilbirds or *guacharo*.

North Coast

The panoramic North Coast Road takes you to one of the Trinidad's most popular beaches. A circular bay with fine white sand backed by rainforested mountains, it's known for its snack stalls selling bake and shark, a delicious fish sandwich. Further east, there's more sun and sand at beautiful **Las Cuevas**; at **Blanchisseuse**, Marianne River holds the **Three Pools** waterfall, and you can hike the **North Coast Bench Trail** to lovely **Paria Bay**, with a waterfall just inland.

Tobago

Tobago takes its name from the tobacco plant, or from the Spanish name for the natives' pipes. The 62,000 Tobagonians like to cultivate their difference from the people of nearby Trinidad. Most of its citizens (90 percent, in fact) are descendants of African slaves, and there is nothing resembling the multiracial mix of the larger island. The folklore, religion and food all find their roots in Africa. Nearly all of Tobago's 42 by 11 km (26 by 7 miles) provides perfect scenery and relaxation. Construction and development of the tourist infrastructure has brought some change to the island, but it has retained much of its primitive aspect and charm.

Scarborough

About 5,000 people live in the capital. Built up a hillside, it clusters around a modern harbour. The busy **market** is overlooked by pretty **Botanical Gardens**.

Fort King George

The island's principal sight, Fort King George was completed in 1779 and offers commanding views of Scarborough, neighbouring Bacolet and across the Atlantic, to Trinidad.

The fort bears witness to French-British rivalry for the island, and a plaque commemorates all the changes in its fortune:

France 1781, Great Britain 1793, and so on. Several bronze cannon remain pointed out over the sea, and the manicured grounds with their mighty saman trees also hold a squat working **lighthouse**. The small **Tobago Museum** is devoted to historical and archaeological collections, with antique charts and Amerindian and colonial artefacts. Downhill from the museum, lie the former prison and the powder magazine, used to store the fort's cache of explosives.

Beaches

Just outside Scarborough, the flat palm-backed sands of **Rockley Bay** are favoured by kitesurfers, while on the other side of the capital, the yellow-sand curve of **Bacolet Beach** was used as a location in the classic Swiss Family Robinson movie.

Southwest

Tobago's southwest tip is home to the majority of the island's resort facilities. Sample the local speciality of curried crab with dumplings from the row of kiosks at **Store Bay Beach**, also a great spot for a swim. For a nominal admission, you can enjoy the spectacular stretch of fine sand and calm turquoise waters at **Pigeon Point**, perfectly placed to watch the sunset and with changing rooms, restaurants and bars.

The nearby **Bon Accord Lagoon** attracts many kinds of birds, and by night you can try a stand-up paddleboard tour of its phosphorescent waters.

The extensive **Buccoo Reef** lies offshore from Pigeon Point and Bon Accord Lagoon. Glass-bottom boats reveal the wonders of the warm tropical sea, and you'll marvel at the queen trigger fish, blue tang, yellowtail, snapper and other beauties of the deep. For a clear view underwater, be sure to make the trip on a fair day at low tide. Snorkel equipment is provided on the boats. The **Nylon Pool** is a sandbar with exceptionally clear water.

Surfers head northeast along the coast to **Mount Irvine Bay**, also perfect for swimming. A resort hotel has tennis courts and an 18-hole championship golf course.

Caribbean Coast

The Northside Road leads northwest of Scarborough to meet the Caribbean coast at Plymouth.

Plymouth

This placid village holds the curious "**Mystery Tombstone**", inscribed in 1783 with an intriguing epitaph in memory of Betty Stiven: "A mother without knowing it, and a wife, without letting her husband know, except by her kind indulgences to him". Islanders translate this as a classic love affair between a master and his black mistress. She was the mother of the man's children, and was honoured by marriage to him only after her death, when the master finally recognized the children. Just beyond lies little **Fort James**, built in 1768, with cannon pointing out over the bay.

Commemorating Tobago's Latvian settlers, the **Great Courland Bay Monument**, situated on a nearby headland, commands a striking view of the sea and of **Turtle Beach**, which offers great swimming and the change to see leatherback turtles nest between March and September. Neighbouring **Stonehaven Bay** is another lovely arc of beach.

Just outside Plymouth lies the **Adventure Farm and Nature Reserve**, a 5-ha (12-acre) tropical estate where you can watch butterflies and throngs of jewel-coloured hummingbirds flocking to the nectar-feeders set up on the balcony. There's also a nature trail through the grounds.

Beaches and Hikes

A winding road sticks close to the coast, as far as Charlotteville. Scenic highlights include precipitous views of headlands and the sea, alternating with picturesque huts on stilts serving as bars, stores or private homes. The largest settlement here is **Castara**, with a cluster of small-scale hotels, guesthouses and restaurants set back from two sandy bays. Tourism is developing here, but the village still relies on fishing, and watching the local men pull in huge seine nets full of fish right from the beach is quite a spectacle. Visitors are welcome to join in!

There is a more remote feel further along the coast at **English-man's Bay**, a ravishing and completely undeveloped beach with excellent snorkelling. Don't miss the roadside lookout point above **Parlatuvier**, a picturesque fishing village enclosed by green hills and with a long pier jutting into the turquoise waters of the bay.

Main Ridge Forest Reserve

Rather than following the coast road to Charlotteville, you can cross through the mountainous interior and the **Main Ridge Forest Reserve** (offering several hiking trails in the rainforest) to Roxborough, over on the Atlantic coast.

Atlantic Coast

The scenic Windward Road travels east from Scarborough, following the wild Atlantic coast. Tiny villages such as **Goodwood**, **Goldsborough** give way to **Roxborough**, the second-largest town on the island. Close by, it is well worth making the short hike to

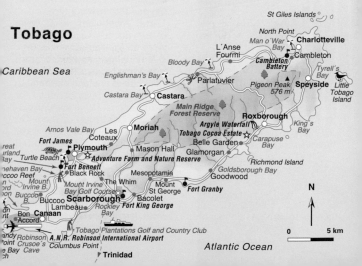

Tobago

Caribbean Sea

St Giles Islands
North Point
Man o' War Bay — Charlotteville
L'Anse Fourmi — Cambleton
Bloody Bay — Cambleton Battery
Englishman's Bay — Parlatuvier — Tyrrell's Bay
Castara Bay — Castara — Pigeon Peak 576 m — Speyside — Little Tobago Island
Main Ridge Forest Reserve
Arnos Vale Bay — Les Coteaux — Moriah — Roxborough — King's Bay
Fort James — Argyle Waterfall — Tobago Cocoa Estate
Plymouth — Mason Hall — Belle Garden — Carapuse Bay
Great Courland Bay — Turtle Beach — Adventure Farm and Nature Reserve — Glamorgan — Richmond Island
Pinehaven Bay — Fort Bennett — Black Rock — Mesopotamia — Goldsborough Bay
Buccoo Reef — Mount Irvine B. — The Whim — Goodwood
Bon Buccoo B. — Mount Irvine Bay Golf Course — Mount St George — Fort Granby
Buccoo — Lambeau — Scarborough — Bacolet
Bon Canaan — Rockley Bay — Fort King George
Accord — Tobago Plantations Golf and Country Club
Sandy Point — A.N.R. Robinson International Airport
Robinson Crusoe's Cave — Columbus Point
Store Bay — Trinidad

N

0 ——— 5 km

Atlantic Ocean

the three-tiered **Argyle Waterfall**, where guides will help you to climb up the side. On a nearby hillside, you can tour **Tobago Cocoa Estate** to learn about cocoa production and taste some of their award-winning chocolate.

Continue to **Speyside**, a scuba-divers' paradise that's known for its reefs studded with huge brain corals. Take a glass-bottom boat tour out to see the reef and visit **Little Tobago**, a 182-ha (450-acre) bird sanctuary, also called Bird-of-Paradise Island (though the birds of paradise were wiped out by Hurricane Flora in 1963). The island supports dry forest and is an important breeding site for seabirds such as terns, red-billed tropicbirds, Audubon's shearwaters and the brown booby.

The Windward Road then crosses the lush vegetation of the tip of the island to **Charlotteville**, a fishing village nestling beneath hills around Man o' War Bay. You can walk around the headland to **Pirate's Bay**, a favourite cove for swimming and with some excellent snorkelling just offshore. On the other side of the village, the remains of **Cambleton Battery** afford sweeping views of the bay.

A golden peach of a beach at Parlatuvier Bay. | **Larger than life and twice as exotic, feathered friends to take home with you.**

hemis.fr/Gardel

hemis.fr

THE HARD FACTS

Climate. Tropical, tempered by northeast trade winds. The hottest season is June–October, the driest November–May. Hurricane season is between mid July and mid October, but the islands are rarely affected. Water temperatures average 29°C and never fall below 25°C.

Communications. The country code for Trinidad and Tobago is 868. Payphones are located in all towns and cities. Roaming costs for using your mobile phone can be high, as can international calls made in hotels, but you can purchase a local SIM card cheaply and easily, and top up credit as you need it. Most hotels and a growing number of cafés and restaurants offer wi-fi, usually for free.

Clothing. For these tropical climes, lightweight, loose clothing is essential, preferably in comfortable cotton; casual styles are the rule. It's advisable to bring along a long-sleeved jacket or cardigan for air-conditioned interiors or cooler evenings. A comfortable pair of sturdy, low-heeled walking shoes is indispensable for excursions.

Currency. Trinidad-Tobago dollar (TT$), divided into 100 cents. Coins from 1 to 50 cents; banknotes from 1 to 100 TT$. The TT$ cannot be converted outside the country. Keep your exchange receipt to reconvert unspent Trinidadian money before you leave. International credit cards are accepted almost everywhere.

Electricity. 115–230 volts AC, 60 Hz. Continental European 2-pin round plugs are common, with variations.

Emergencies. Call 999 for the police, 990 for fire service and 811 for an ambulance.

Time. UTC/GMT –4, all year round.

Tipping. Hotel restaurants usually add a service charge of 10 percent to the bill; if this is not the case, a tip of 10–15 percent is customary.

Water. Tap water is chlorinated, but it's best to drink bottled mineral water, especially in rural areas.

An iconic fofoti (mangrove) tree on Eagle Beach in Aruba.

istockphoto.com/Tran

ABC ISLANDS
ARUBA, BONAIRE, CURAÇAO

The former Netherlands islands of Aruba, Bonaire and Curaçao are situated in the warm waters of the southern Caribbean, all at a distance of less than 80 km (50 miles) north of the Venezuelan coast. The ABC islands are the three westernmost islands of the Leeward Antilles, a chain of islands which also includes the Venezuelan islands of La Tortuga and Margarita.

Aruba

There are many reasons for visiting the honeymoon capital of the Caribbean. You'll find water sports galore, shopping bargains from all over the world, attractive scenery, spicy Indonesian food, friendly people—and glorious white sand beaches. Snorkelling and scuba fans appreciate Aruba's warm, clear waters teeming with vivid tropical fish. There are spectacular coral formations and even a few sunken vessels to be seen. You may want to try out a typically Aruban pastime: cart-sailing.

The island is only 32 km (20 miles) long by 10 km (6 miles) wide. From the capital, Oranjestad ("Orange Town"), there's a well-maintained coastal road and a network of secondary roads through the interior.

Oranjestad

The island's lovely old Dutch-gabled capital is situated on the southwestern coast. Walk along the wharf to the old schooner harbour. A lively open-air market takes place each morning, with fresh fish, fruit and vegetables sold directly from the boats.

Wilhelminastraat is a veritable showcase for the 18th century Oranjestad: tall, narrow-gabled buildings with red-tiled roofs, painted in cool pastels, intense yellows and royal blues, stuccoed with white decoration. This appealing chocolate-box architectural style can be seen throughout all the islands that formed the Netherlands Antilles.

On nearby Schelpstraat the **National Archaeological Museum Aruba** has a collection of more than 10,000 Amerindian artefacts of shell, stone and bone.

ABC ISLANDS FLASHBACK

15th–16th centuries

Alonso de Ojeda discovers Aruba and Curaçao in 1499, claiming it for Spain. A Spanish landing party from Amerigo Vespucci's expedition discovers the Bonaire, where the Dutch succeed the Spanish in 1623 and start producing salt. The Netherlands West India Company takes Curaçao in 1634; the island becomes the main Dutch trading base in the region. Two years later, the Dutch take over Aruba with little opposition from the Spanish. Peter Stuyvesant is appointed governor of Aruba and the other Dutch islands from 1643 to 1647, but spends most of these years on Curaçao.

19th century–present

The British occupy the ABCs at the beginning o the 19th century, finally returning them to the Dutch. Slavery is abolished in 1863.

Aruba and five other Dutch-speaking islands form the autonomous federation of the Netherlands Antilles in 1954. Aruba secedes from the federation in 1986 and remains an autonomous part of the kingdom of the Netherlands. The federation is dissolved on October 10, 2010. Curaçao and five other islands win autonomy from the Netherlands in 1954 to form the Netherlands Antilles; Willemstad is chosen as its capital. Bonaire becomes a special municipality within the country of the Netherlands.

istockphoto.com/Sprada

Fort Zoutman to the east was built in 1796 and is the oldest building in Oranjestad. A lighthouse, the Willem III Tower, was added in 1870 to serve as a lookout against pirates.

It now houses a historical museum and hosts the Bon Bini festival each Tuesday evening, featuring local crafts, food and music.

Shops cluster around **Caya G.F. Betico Croes**. Since there's no sales tax in Aruba, you can find some real bargains in luxury articles all over the world.

There are also several excellent **shopping malls**: head for the Renaissance Marketplace and Royal Plaza Mall near the cruiseship port, and the nearby Port of Call Marketplace.

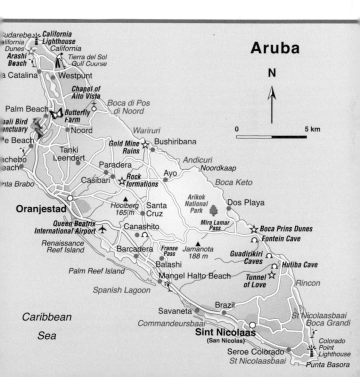

Renaissance Island Aruba

You can take a boat to this private island just off the coast, have lunch at the hotel and visit the secluded **Flamingo Beach**, where real flamingos patrol the sands.

West Coast

Take a leisurely drive up the west coast, passing the fine white sands of hotel-lined **Eagle Beach**, one of the best on the island.

A short way north is **De Olde Molen**, a windmill built in Holland in 1804, shipped across the Atlantic and reconstructed here in 1960; it's now a restaurant, with lovely views from its terrace.

Just opposite are the wetlands of the **Bubali Bird Sanctuary**, populated by cormorants, herons, fish eagles and brown pelicans. More than 80 different migratory species flock to the area.

Inland of gleaming **Palm Beach**, the landscaped gardens at **Butterfly Farm** are home to many species of butterfly. You can take a guided walk or explore independently.

Hadicurari (also known as **Fisherman's Huts**) is a beach of powdery white sand, where constant offshore winds provide ideal conditions for windsurfing. Off the coast, the wreck of *SS Antilla*, a World War II German freighter, attracts scuba divers.

To the north, **Arashi Beach** is a calm and sheltered spot, ideal for snorkelling.

At the northwestern tip of the island, take a walk around **California Dunes**, the windy and barren site of an old lighthouse named after the *California*, a US ship that sank two years before the lighthouse was built in 1910. Sunset here is spectacular.

Noord

Heading back to the capital, take the road that leads inland to Noord and **St Ann's Church**, where you can see a lovely hand-carved oak altar, the work of a 19th-century Dutch artisan. If you have time, make a detour to the tiny **Alto Vista chapel**, with stone pews outside. It dates from 1952 but stands on the site of an earlier chapel put up by the Spanish.

From Noord, the road travels back to Oranjestad through the *cunucu*, as the countryside is called in Papiamento, dotted with brightly coloured houses, patches of cacti, enormous boulders and the emblematic *divi divi* trees, bent double by the trade winds.

The Interior and the East

Some of Aruba's most popular sights lie inland, within easy reach of Oranjestad.

Rock Gardens

At **Casibari** and the nearby **Hooiberg** ("Haystack Mountain"), you can see "rock gardens" — huge boulders weighing thousands of tons scattered as if thrown about by some crazed giant. Several of the boulders are engraved with ritual Indian carvings, centuries old, made by the early inhabitants, Caribs or Arawaks. The Hooiberg is not Aruba's tallest peak, but it features a long flight of steps that takes you 165 m to the top—a breathtaking look-out.

There are more rock gardens at **Ayo**, and from here you can continue to the north coast and the ghost town of **Bushiribana** with its abandoned gold mine. Gold was discovered here in 1824 and was mined for nearly a century. Close to Bushribana, the **Aruba Ostrich Farm** is a rather unusual attraction: during the guided tour you get to touch and even feed these enormous birds.

Balashi
The ghost town of Balashi was the centre of a profitable gold mining area in the 19th century. You can visit the abandoned mine and the ruins of a gold-smeltery.

Continue to **Frenchman's Pass** in the Aruba uplands, the haunt of the huge green parakeet, a species that can be found exclusively in this part of the Caribbean.

Arikok National Park
East of the town of Santa Cruz, **Mira Lamar Pass** nestles between Aruba's two highest peaks: Arikok, 176 m, and Jamanota,

188 m. The road rises to give some excellent views. This area, alongside some 20 percent of the entire island, comes under the boundaries of **Arikok National Park**, whose rugged coastline and cacti-strewn hillsides provide a habitat for a rich array of wildlife.

The park also holds a number of caves, decorated with Indian drawings and thought to have figured in ancient sacrificial rites.

At **Guadirikiri Caves**, honeymooners may be intrigued by signs pointing out the **Tunnel of Love**, a large cave with a heart-shaped entrance, coloured walls and a resident bat colony. Along the coast, **Fontein** caves are Indian pictographs and graffiti left by early European settlers.

East at **Dos Playa** and **Boca Prins**, you'll have a once-in-a-lifetime chance to try the unusual Aruban sport of dune-sliding. To the north, there's safe swimming at **Conchi Natural Pool**, a natural rock-pool on this wild stretch of coast. There's an informative **visitor centre** at the San Fuego entrance.

San Nicolas (Sint Nicolaas)
Back on the coast road, you can continue to Aruba's second-largest city, San Nicolas, at the island's southwest tip. This modern community was built for the workers of Aruba's giant Lago Oil Refinery. East is the **Seroe Colorado** area, famous for its beaches.

Bonaire

Bonaire boasts some of the loveliest fringing reefs in the Caribbean—and more flamingos than people. Because of the abundant coral growth and variety of fish, the Netherlands Antilles National Parks Foundation has established a programme for reef protection. Some 40 km (24 miles) long and surrounded by crystal-clear waters, the whole island forms a natural sanctuary, officially protected as the Bonaire Marine Park and home to a stunningly diverse range of coral and sealife. Experts rate it one of the world's top spots for snorkelling and scuba-diving. Collection of black coral or other corals is allowed only for the Handicrafts Foundation. Forty diving spots have been designated and mooring buoys placed to prevent anchor damage to the reefs.

Kralendijk

The island curves round with its back to the trade winds, sheltering the tiny capital of Kralendijk in the central crook of its western curve. Across the natural harbour lies the uninhabited rocky islet of Little Bonaire, a favourite picnic and diving spot.

Kralendijk means "coral dike", and it is easy to see why: the beaches that sweep away to north and south are edged by coral reefs running out 90 m into the blue-green sea. The town's population of 3,000 live in trim colour-washed houses set in neat gardens. By the harbour, the **fish market** is housed in a miniature Greek temple. Nearby, **Fort Oranje** displays a 150-year-old cannon. The **Bonaire Museum**, 7 Kaya van de Ree, Sabana, is worth a visit to see artefacts from Bonaire homes and to learn something of the island's early history.

Island Sights

Bonaire, is the driest island in the Caribbean, strewn with cactus and prickly pear. The south is sandy and flat, running down to salt pans, while the north is covered with rocky acacia-clad hills, culminating in 240-m Mount Brandaris. Those who want to snorkel or scuba-dive will head straight to Lac Bay, and there's no lack of choice for beaches, *playas* and *bokas* for those who prefer swimming and sailing. If you prefer to stay dry, take a day-trip right round the island, and a tour over the reefs in a glass-bottomed boat.

Washington Slagbaai National Park

Covering 5,643-ha (13,944 -acre) of northwest Bonaire, with **Mount Brandaris** as its centre point, the park encompasses sand dunes, beaches, wetlands and dry forests that are home to around 200 bird species, including parrots, parakeets and hummingbirds. There's a visitor centre at the main entrance north of Rincón. **Gotomeer** is a blue salt lake where brilliant roseate flamingos feeding long-legged in the shallows. Occasionally great flocks of the birds take off, unravelling like a piece of pink knitting and circling round to land again and resume their feast of algae.

Rincón

The village was once the home of black slaves who worked in the salt pans. From here you can visit **Boca Onima** on the northeast coast to view shallow caves with rock carvings coloured in red, the work of the original Indian inhabitants and estimated to be more than 500 years old. Archaeologists have so far failed to decipher them.

Lac Bay

An arc of mangroves curves round the lagoon at Lac Bay, where the fishermen harvest conch and leave the shells piled up on the beach. This is the ideal spot for a swim in safe, clear water—or a trip in a glass-bottomed boat. Seas wash in and out over a coral reef into a bay, making it the perfect nursery for fish and a favourite diving spot. Offshore winds also make it a major centre for windsurfing; lessons and equipment are available.

Huter/Gräfenhain

Flamingos at lunch in the salt flats of Pekelmeer.

Flamingo Sanctuary

On **Pekelmeer**, you will find one of the largest colonies of flamingos in the western hemisphere, numbering over 10,000 and comprising a stunning sight for the visitor. In spring, these amazing birds build their round mud nests and raise their young on the salt flats where the local salt company has set aside a reserve of 50 ha (125 acres). Watch them sieving water through their hooked beaks to feed on the brine shrimps and algae which give them their startling pink colour.

DINING AND SHOPPING

On the menu

Visitors to Aruba and Bonaire will find a mix of international restaurants, specialising in Indonesian food but catering for every kind of palate.

Sopito, the tasty fish and coconut soup flavoured with salt pork and assorted spices, is an excellent way to start your meal.

If you're really hungry, try *keshi yena*, Edam cheese stuffed with meat or fish and raisins.

Aruba's best-known dish is *stoba*, a highly seasoned lamb or goat stew, often served with banana fritters. Marinated conch is a very popular dish on Bonaire. Conch ragu, especially the one made with the giant conch from Lac Bay, is delicious.

You should not miss the authentic Indonesian *rijsttafel*, the famous array of several different dishes served with rice. Highlights include such delights as *ikan asem manis* (sweet-sour fish), *babi ketjap* (pork cooked in sweet soy sauce), *semur sapi* (beef stew with tomatoes) and so on. *Nasi goreng* is a sampling of dishes from the *rijsttafel*.

All the famous Dutch beers are available, as well as Aruba's own Balashi.

You might like to try Aruba's very own liqueur, *cucui*. Made from the leaves of the aloe plant, this red, licorice-flavoured liqueur dates back to the times of the Arawak Indians.

Curaçao is the home of the famed curaçao orange liqueur, distilled from a secret recipe. Blue curaçao is used for colourful cocktails, which are very popular. Dutch brandy is milder than its French counterpart, cognac.

The best buys

Aruba's shops promise the latest in designer fashions from Italy and France. Oranjestad, the capital, is a tax-free port, so you may happen upon considerable bargaining. Also look out for Royal Copenhagen porcelain, Hummel figurines, Delft faience, and Swedish crystal.

Bonaire puts the flamingo motif onto T-shirts and tea-towels. It is also known for its earrings, necklaces and bracelets made from local shells.

In Curaçao, don't forget to buy some Indonesian spices and curaçao liqueur.

The **Willemstoren Lighthouse**, (also known as Lacre Punt Light) was built in 1837; it is well maintained and in good working order. It rises on the coast just before you reach the main salt pans ringed by pyramids of white salt. The salt is deposited by the sea in ponds and dried into crystals by sun and wind.

Three tall stone obelisks on the shore in the Dutch colours of red, white and blue once guided ships to their moorings by the ponds. Along the beach, the remains of 19th-century **slave huts** have been restored. The slaves worked here all week and at weekends trekked 24 km (15 miles) across the island to their homes in Rincón.

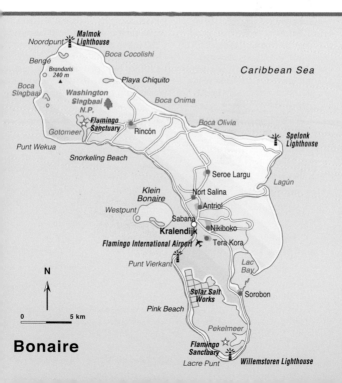

Bonaire

Curaçao

A fragment of Amsterdam set adrift in the West Indies, Willemstad is the most European of Caribbean cities. Curaçaoans seem particularly adept at reconciling old-world charm with the business-like present. Lovely 18th-century Dutch colonial houses look out over St Anna Bay, while cruise ships and oil tankers glide by on their way to the busy port. The island, 60 km (38 miles) long and 12 km (7 miles) wide, has a population of 153,500, made up of different nationalities. In the countryside, you will find scattered windmills, some old Dutch plantation houses and a good deal of arid, windy land with cactus and divi-divi trees.

Willemstad

The old center of Willemstad, the capital city of Curaçao, has been a UNESCO World Heritage site since 1997. Right through the middle of Willemstad runs Sint Annabaai (St Anna Bay), an inlet connecting the Caribbean with the Schottegat deep-water port.

Sint Annabaai

On the east side of the inlet is the **Punda**, the city's oldest district, while on the west is the **Otrabanda** ("the other side"). Edged with fine Dutch colonial houses, the bustling bay provides the best show in town. A never-ending procession of small sailing boats,

sleek cruise ships and lumbering oil tankers parades back and forth between Schottegat and the Caribbean Sea, with spectators nearly always around to watch the ships.

Queen Emma Bridge, a floating pontoon bridge that swings open on a hinge to let the ships by, was the ingenious idea of an enterprising American, Leonard B. Smith, the same man who brought ice and electricity to Curaçao. At first, back in 1888, they charged a toll: 2¢ for those wearing shoes but free for the barefooted, the laudable intention being to tax only those with the means to pay. However, it seems, the poor often borrowed or bought sandals so they could pay, while the well-heeled (financially speaking) liked to take off their shoes and cross for nothing. The authorities eventually gave up and now everyone goes over free, shoes or not.

For many years, the Queen Emma was the bay's only bridge, and every time it opened for ships the road traffic backed up for miles. In 1974, an arching, four-lane bridge was inaugurated for vehicular traffic. With its 56-m high span, the **Queen Juliana Bridge** allows all but the tallest ships to sail right under it.

The buildings along St Anna Bay house elegant shops and restaurants. The Dutch imprint

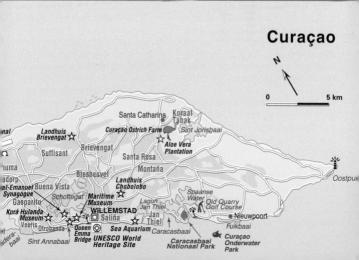

Curaçao

here is unmistakable: narrow, gabled, three- and four-storey structures with red-tiled roofs. The tiles were brought over the ocean as ballast on ships; for the return trip the vessels were filled with salt that the Dutch used to cure herring.

As for the rainbow colours of the 18th-century houses—the cool pastels, the vibrant yellows and blues—we have an early governor of Curaçao to thank. The poor man suffered from ferocious headaches, and the glare of the tropical sun on the white buildings hurt his eyes. So he ordered that every house be painted any colour but white.

Punda
Near the pontoon bridge on the Punda side, the lovely golden yellow **Penha & Sons Building**, with white trim, is one of the city's oldest houses (1708). It sits at the corner of the two main shopping streets, Breedestraat and Heerenstraat.

Two forts guarded the entrance to St Anna Bay. On the east side, the **Waterfort** was built in 1634; it's now a hotel but the cannons remain.

Fort Amsterdam
Imposing mustard walls surround Fort Amsterdam, the historic centre of Willemstad. Construction probably began before 1642, when Governor Peter Stuyvesant was in residence. Now it's the seat of government. The complex of buildings consists of various offices, the **Governor's Residence**—a gracious Dutch colonial mansion with 19th-century additions—and the **Fort Church**, the oldest in the island (1769), which has a British cannonball lodged in one of its walls and is worth seeing for its small museum and lovely stained-glass windows.

Mikvé Israel-Emanuel Synagogue
Dating from 1732, the Dutch colonial synagogue, right in the middle of the shopping district, is the oldest in the Western Hemisphere. Its congregation was founded 1650 by a dozen families of Sephardic Jews who came to Curaçao from Amsterdam. Yellow outside, richly furnished within, the synagogue has four magnificent bronze chandeliers, replicas of the ones in Amsterdam's Portuguese Synagogue. The floor is very striking—a carpet of white sand, symbolizing the desert where the Jews wandered in their search for the Promised Land.

The **Joods Historisch Cultureel Museum** (Jewish Historical Museum) was once a rabbi's home and later a Chinese laundry. But the discovery of a 300-year-old *mikvah*, or ritual bath, in the courtyard led to extensive restoration of the 18th-century house. The museum contains many valuable historical objects linked with Jewish ritual.

Postal Museum
At the corner of Kuiperstraat and former Keukenstraat, this bright red building with a pointed gable is Punda's oldest townhouse, dating from 1693 and restored in 1990. It displays stamps from all over the world.

Floating Market
Try to visit the market in the morning, when it's most lively. Small boats from Venezuela bring fresh produce and fish, returning home after they have sold their merchandise. Haggling is still the order of the day— whether you're buying a piece of fabric or some exotic fruit.

Scharloo
The **Wilhelminabrug** (drawbridge) leads to Scharloo, where you'll see some of the finest homes in Willemstad, ranging from early colonial to Victorian. The area is also home to an excellent **Maritime Museum**, with an interior that looks like the inside of a ship and displays which explain the island's relationship with the sea. Up on a hill here, the **Roosevelt House**, with its black-tiled roof and American flag, is the official

wikimedia.org/Baselmans

Take your time to watch, smell and why not to paint the floating market.

residence of the US Consul General. You will find the very best view of Willemstad at **Fort Nassau**, 60 m above the inner harbour. From the fort or its restaurant you can look down on the city below. In the distance you can also see the gigantic oil refinery.

Kurá Hulanda Museum
In the Hulanda District, a Dutch plantation house set in former slave quarters, this is one of the Caribbean's most engaging museums. Focused around African

heritage, the displays include a fascinating and moving section on slavery and the slave trade, with an interesting collection of colonial furnishings and relics of the Caiquietio Indian culture.

Curaçao Sea Aquarium

One of Willemstad's star attractions is the aquarium complex, stretching along the largest beach on Curaçao. You can enjoy a diversity of sea-life, take a trip in a glass-bottom boat, swim with dolphins or sea lions, snorkel with rays and hand-feed sharks. The complex also offers water sports, shops and restaurants.

Island Sights

As you travel around the island, you will see some fine old Dutchor plantation houses, or *landhuizen*.

Landhuis Chobolobo

Curaçao's unique liqueur is made at this yellow-painted 17th-century *landhuis* in Salinja. Self-guided tours of the distillery include a film screening which explains production process, and are followed by a tasting session. Curaçao is made with the fragrant peel of a green citrus (*laraha*) that grows only on this island, and gives the liqueur its distinctive flavour; the fruit is like a very bitter orange, considered inedible.

Christoffel National Park

This park is a spacious preserve criss-crossed by marked walking trails. You can climb 375 m **Mount Christoffel** or stay closer to sea level and observe the birds and deer, and the stands of cactus and aloe. At the entrance, the buildings of a 17th-century *landhuis* hold the **Savonet Museum**, which gives some background on island history and the park's geology, fauna and flora.

To the west of the park, **Playa Lagún** has a beautiful, secluded beach. A short way inland and atop a hill which affords some stunning views, the restored **Landhuis Kenepa** was once the centre of a sugar estate, and saw a significant slave rebellion in 1795. It now holds the **Museo Tula**, where displays give insight into plantation life and African heritage.

Hato Caves

Take a guided tour through these easy-access caves, where stalactites and stalagmites given the star treatment through lighting effects.

Curaçao Ostrich Farm

This working farm offers the chance to pet and feed ostriches, or take a quad-bike tour of the local area. On the way, stop off at the **Aloe Vera Plantation** to learn about this cure-all plant and buy some aloe products.

THE HARD FACTS

Climate. The islands have warm, rarely overly-hot weather year-round, with average temperatures most often between 24° and 29°C (75° and 85°F). Trade winds can be fierce.

Clothing. Take light clothing made of cotton or linen. A lightweight sweater is useful for the cooler evenings

Communications. Area codes are as follows: Aruba (297); Bonaire (599); Curacao (5999). Roaming costs for using your own mobile phone are high in all the islands; local SIM cards are cheap and widely available. Wi-fi is available free from cafés and restaurants in all island resorts.

Credit cards and travellers cheques. International credit cards are widely accepted by most hotels, better restaurants and shops. Travellers cheques are also accepted, preferably those in US dollars or Euros.

Currency. Curaçao's currency is the Netherlands Antilles florin or guilder (NAf), divided into 100 cents. Coins: from 1 cent to 5 NAf. Notes: 10 to 100 NAf. The Aruba florin or guilder (AFl, AWG) is divided into 100 cents. Coins range from 5 cents to 5 AFl, banknotes from 10 to 500 AFl. Prices are usually quoted in the local currency, but shops also accept US dollars and euros. The official currency of Bonaire is the US dollar.

Emergencies. Aruba: police 100; fire service and ambulance 911; Bonaire: 911 for all services; Curacao: police and fire service 911, ambulance 912.

Language. The official languages are Dutch and Papiamento, a mixture of Dutch, Spanish, Portuguese and English, French, Carib Indian and West African dialects. Many locals also speak English and Spanish.

Time. UTC/GMT−4, all year round.

Tipping. Most hotel and restaurant bills include a service charge (10–15%). If not, a tip of 10–20% is expected.

Water. Bottled mineral water is advised.

Nassau

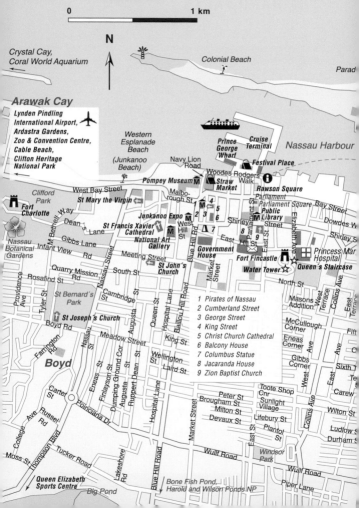

0   1 km

N

Crystal Cay,
Coral World Aquarium

Colonial Beach

Parad

Arawak Cay

**Lynden Pindling
International Airport,** ✈
**Ardastra Gardens,
Zoo & Convention Centre,
Cable Beach,
Clifton Heritage
National Park**

Western
Esplanade
Beach
(Junkanoo
Beach)

Nassau Harbour

Prince
George
Wharf

Cruise
Terminal

Navy Lion
Road

Festival Place

Woodes Rodgers
Walk

Pompey Museum 🅜

**Straw
Market**

Rawson Square

Malbo-
rough St

West Bay Street

St Mary the Virgin

Parliament

Parliament Square
Bay Street

Clifford
Park

**Fort
Charlotte**

Junkanoo Expo

West
Hill
St

Shirley

**Public
Library**

Parliament
Street

Dowdes W

Dean
Lane

**St Francis Xavier
Cathedral**

**National Art
Gallery**

East

Hill St

Shirley S

Gibbs Lane

Infant View
Rd

Meeting Street

**St John's
Church**

**Government
House**

Fort Fincastle

**Princess Mar
Hospital**

Queen's Staircase

Nassau
Botanical
Gardens

Quarry Mission
Rd

South St

Market
Street

**Water
Tower** ☆

North St

Rosalind St

Cambridge
St

1 Pirates of Nassau
2 Cumberland Street
3 George Street
4 King Street
5 Christ Church Cathedral
6 Balcony House
7 Columbus Statue
8 Jacaranda House
9 Zion Baptist Church

Masons
Addition

West
Terrace

East
Terrace

**St Bernard's
Park**

Hospital Lane

Queen
St

Ballou Rd

McCullough
Corner

Eneas
Corner

Fift

C

Boyd Rd

St Joseph's Church

Meadow Street

Augusta
St

King St

Wellington
St

Laird St

Gibbs
Corner

Sixth T

East

Te

Providence
Ave

Tyler St

Nassau Street

Dumping Ground Cor

Ruppert Dean

Carew

Farrington
Rd

Boyd

Carter
St

Russel
Rd

Poinciana Dr

Finlayson St

Eneas
St

Market Street

Toote Shop
Cnr
Sunlight
Village

Peter St

Brougham St

Milton St

Devaux St

Lifebury St

Plantol
St

Wilton St

Collins Ave

Ludlow S

Durham S

College

Moss St

Thompson Blvd

Ave

Lakeshore
Rd

Blue Hill Road

Wulff Road

Bone Fish Pond,
Harold and Wilson Ponds NP

East
St

Windsor
Park

Wulff Road

Piper Lane

**Queen Elizabeth
Sports Centre**

Big Pond

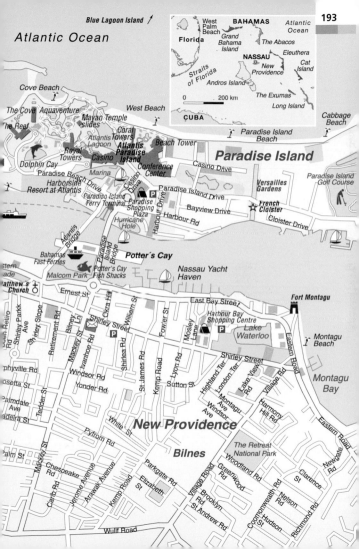

Blue Lagoon Island

Atlantic Ocean

BAHAMAS

West Palm Beach

Atlantic Ocean

Florida

Grand Bahama Island

The Abacos

NASSAU

Eleuthera

New Providence

Cat Island

Straits of Florida

Andros Island

The Exumas

0   200 km

Long Island

CUBA

Cove Beach

The Cove Aquaventure

West Beach

Mayan Temple Slides

The Reef

Cabbage Beach

Atlantis Towers

Coral Towers

Beach Tower

Paradise Island Beach

Paradise Island

Atlantis Lagoon

Royal Towers

Atlantis Paradise Island

Casino

Dolphin Cay

Conference Center

Casino Drive

Paradise Beach

Harborside Resort at Atlantis

Marina

Casino Drive

Paradise Island Drive

Versailles Gardens

Paradise Island Golf Course

Paradiso Island Ferry Terminal

Paradise Shopping Plaza

Paradise Island Drive

Bayview Drive

French Cloister

Hurricane Hole

Harbour Rd

Cloister Drive

Atlantis Bridge

Paradise Island Bridge

Potter's Cay

Bahamas Fast Ferries

Malcom Park

Potter's Cay Fish Shacks

Nassau Yacht Haven

stern ade

Matthew's Church

Ernest St.

Okra Hill

William St.

East Bay Street

Fowler St.

Harbour Bay Shopping Centre

Lake Waterloo

Fort Montagu

Montagu Beach

Shirley Park Ave

Shirley Slope

Birley St.

Shirley Street

Mackey St.

Ivanhoe Rd

Shirlea Rd

St James Rd

Mosley Lane

Shirley Street

Eastern Road

Montagu Bay

Retirement Rd

Windsor Rd

Kemp Road

Sutton St.

Highland Ter.

London Ter.

Lake-View Rd

Village Rd

Rosetta St.

Yonder Rd

Lyon Rd

Montagu Ave

Harmony Hill Rd

phyville Rd

Tedder St.

New Providence

Windsor Ave

Palmdale Ave

White St.

Bilnes

Village Road

The Retreat National Park

adeira St

Pyfrom Rd

Woodland Rd

Greenwood Rd

Clarence St

Newgate Rd

alm St

Mackey St.

Chespeake Rd

Parkgate Rd

Elizabeth

Brooklyn

St Andrew Rd

Commonwealth Rd

Nelson St

Hudson St

Richmond Rd

Carib Rd

Jerome Avenue

Arawak Avenue

Kemp Road

Village Road

Wulff Road

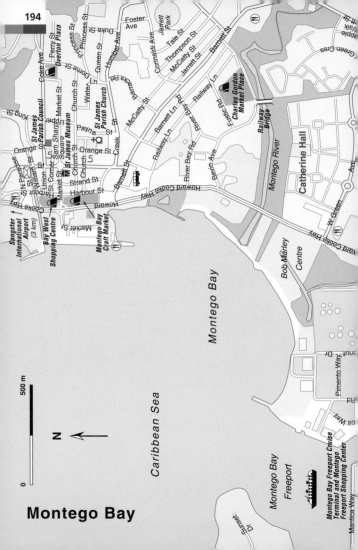

Montego Bay

Caribbean Sea

Montego Bay

Montego Bay

Montego Bay Freeport

Foster Ave

Jarrett Park

Duke St

Tale St

Thompson St

McCatty St

Jarrett St

Barnett St

Perry St

Princess St

Dome St

Queen St

Humber Ave

Corniddi Ave

Cdrol Ave

Overton Plaza

Church St

Water St

Railway Ln

Charles Gordon Market Place

Railway Bridge

McCatty St

Barnett Ln

Barnett Ln

Railway Ln

River Bay Rd

Eustic Rd

St James Parish Church

Montego River

Catherine Hall

King St

St James Parish Council

Orange St

N Paradise St

Union St

William St

Market St

Church St

Market St

Payne St

San Shara Market St

St James Square

St James Museum

Church St

Orange St

Church St

Strand St

Barnett St

Creek

Bevin Ave

Howard Cooke Hwy

Sangster International Airport (3 km)

Cooke Hwy

Harbour St

Bay West Shopping Centre

Market St

Montego Bay Craft Market

Howard Cooke HWY

W Green Ave

Yard Cooke HWY

Bob Marley Centre

Pimento Way

Anut

Dr

St

Way

Sunset Dr

Manticho Way

Montego Bay Freeport Cruise Terminal and Montego Freeport Shopping Center

N ←

500 m

0

La Romana

N
0   600 m

Aeropuerto Internacional Bayahibe, Higüey

Casa de Campo & Altos de Chavón
Casa de Campo

Aeropuerto La Romana

Terminal de Cruceros de la Romana

Caribbean Sea

Autopista del Este

URBANIZACIÓN BUENA VISTA

Río Dulce

BARRIO LA CALETA

Francisco Richiez

Fco Castillo Marquez

García Dickson

Bienvenido Creales

Enriquillo

D Teofilo Ferry

García Lupeñón

Héctor René Gil

Fray Juan

Gregorio Lupeñón

Iglesia Santa Rosa de Lima

Parque Central

Duarte

El Obelisco

Dr Teofilo Ferry

Hernandez

Av. Santa Rosa

URBANIZACIÓN VILLA VERDE

URBANIZACIÓN LAS PIEDRAS

Pedro

Espaillat

Mercado Municipal

Pedro

Eugenio A. Miranda

Pedro

Teofilo

Espaillat

CENTRO

Pedro

ENSANCHE LA HOZ

C-1RA

Padre Abreu

Luis Joaquín Suárez

Calle A

Calle B

Tiburcio M. Lopez

Gaston Fdo

Eugenio A. Delince

Duarte

Av. 30 de Mayo

Barreto Payan

Av. Libertad

C-1RA

C-2DA

Pedro

María Trinidad Sánchez

José Padua

Calle 1RA

Héctor René Gil

Héctor PQ

Héctor PQ

CENTRAL ROMANA

Concepción Bona

Do Abril

María Montez

Palo Hincado

Guido Gil

Independencia

De Abril

Julio A García

C-1RA

ENSANCHE PEREYRA

C-3

C-4

Fray Juan

Eugenio A. Miranda

Duarte

ENSANCHE MIRAMAR

C-1

C-2

ENSANCHE CHICAGO

Dr Teofilo Hernandez

Juana Saltitopa

Sagrario Díaz

Av. Padre Abreu

Gregorio

Lupeñón

Lupeñón

C-2

C-1RA

RP Lupeñón

Av. 30 de Marzo

Av. Circunvalación

C-M

Cueva de Las Maravillas

Autopista del Este

ENSANCHE VILLA ROLL

C-E

C-D

C-A

C-3RA

C-4TA

C-3RA

C-A

C-2DA

C-F

C-H

C-G

C-1RA

Guacanagarix

Mayobanex

URBANIZACIÓN QUISQUEYA

C-3RA

M-20

M-21

M-22

M-23

M-24

M-25

Av. Circunvalación

Santo Domingo

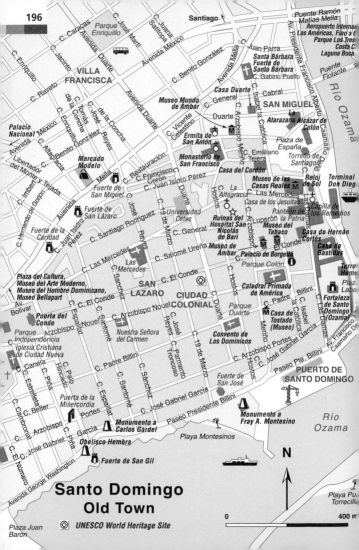

Santo Domingo
Old Town

 UNESCO World Heritage Site

0   400 m

N

Santiago

Parque
Enriquillo

VILLA
FRANCISCA

Puente Ramón
Matías Mella
Av. Presidente Francisco Aeropuerto Internac
Las Américas, Faró a A
Parque Los Tres
Costa C
Laguna Boca

Puente
Flotante

Río Ozama

Palacio
Nacional

Mercado
Modelo

Fuerte de
San Miguel

Fuerte de
San Lázaro

Fuerte de
la Caridad

Museo Mundo
de Ámbar

Santa Bárbara
Fuerte de
Santa Bárbara

Casa Duarte

SAN MIGUEL

Ermita de
San Antón

Monasterio de
San Francisco

Casa del Cordón

La
Altagracia

Universidad
Cetec

Ruinas del
Hospital San
Nicolás de Bari

La Atarazana Alcázar de
Colón

Plaza de
España

Torreón de
Santiago

Museo de las
Casas Reales

Casa de los Jesuitas

Panteón de
la Patria

Museo del
Tabaco

Reloj
de Sol

Terminal
Don Dieg

Capilla de
los Remedios

Casa de Hernán
Cortés

Casa de
Bastidas

Museo de
Ámbar

Palacio de Borgellá

Parque Colón

Plaza del Cultura,
Museo del Arte Moderno,
Museo del Hombre Dominicano,
Museo Bellapart

SAN
LÁZARO

CIUDAD
COLONIAL

Catedral Primada
de América

Torre
Home

Casa
Laba

Fortaleza
de Santo
Domingo
(Ozama)

Puerta del
Conde

Parque
Independencia
Iglesia Cristiana
de Ciudad Nueva

Nuestra Señora
del Carmen

Casa de
Tostado
(Museo)

Parque
Duarte

Convento de
Los Dominicos

Puerta de la
Misericordia

PUERTO DE
SANTO DOMINGO

Fuerte de
San José

Monumento a
Carlos Gardel

Obelisco Hembra

Fuerte de San Gil

Monumento a
Fray A. Montesino

Playa Montesinos

Río
Ozama

Plaza Juan
Barón

Playa Pu
Torrecille

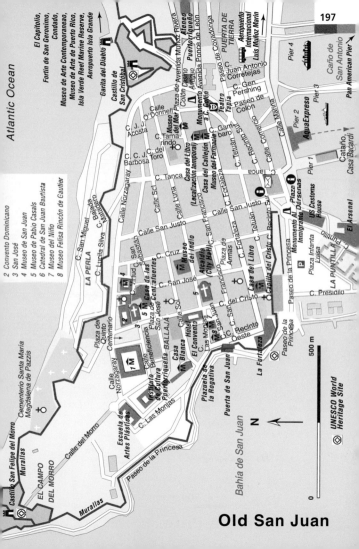

Old San Juan

Atlantic Ocean

El Capitolio,
Fortín de San Geronimo,
Condado,
Museo de Arte Contemporaneao,
Museo de Arte de Puerto Rico,
Isla Verde Reef Marine Reserve,
Aeropuerto Isla Grande

2 Convento Dominicano
3 San José
4 Museo de San Juan
5 Museo de Pablo Casals
6 Catedral de San Juan Bautista
7 Museo del Niño
8 Museo Felisa Rincón de Cautier

Castillo San Felipe del Morro
Cementerio Santa Maria
Magdalena de Pazzis

Garita del Diablo
Castillo de San Cristóbal

Ateneo
Puertorriqueño
Casino Antiguo
Colón
Teatro
Tapia

Aeropuerto
Internacional
Luis Muñoz Marín

Pier 4

Caño de San Antonio

Pan American Pier

AquaExpreso

Pier 3

C. Gen. Pershing

Pier 2

Pier 1

Cataño,
Casa Bacardí

US Customs House

El Arsenal

LA PUNTILLA

La Puntilla

Bahía de San Juan

LA PERLA

EL CAMPO
DEL MORRO

Murallas

Escuela de
Artes Plásticas

Calle del Morro

Murallas

Paseo de la Princesa

Plaza del
Quinto
Centenario

Instituto
de Cultura
Puertorriqueña

BALLAJÁ

Casa
Blanca

El Convento

Plazuela de
la Rogativa

Puerta de San Juan

La Fortaleza

Paseo de la Princesa

Plaza Infanta
Luisa

C. Presidillo

Plaza de la Princesa

Monumento Al
Immigrante

Plaza
Al Dársenas

Casa del Libro

Capilla del Cristo

Casa del Cristo

Alcaldia
(City Hall)

Plaza de
Armas

Casa de las
Contrafuertes

Museo del
Indio

San José

Plaza de
San José

Calle Norzagaray

Calle Lucila Silva

Balada
Matadero

Calle San Miguel

Calle Sol

Calle Luna

Calle Tanca

C. San
Sebastián

C. San José

Calle San Justo

C. Cruz

C. del Cristo

C. San Francisco

C. Fortaleza

C. Tetuán

C. Recinto Sur

C. San Justo

Calle Norzagaray

C. J. J. Acosta

C. del Toro

C. C. J. C. del Barbosa

C. Tamarindo

C. O'Donnell

Plaza de Avenida Muñoz Rivera

Monumento A. Colón

Avenida Ponce de León

Paseo de Covadonga

Museo del Mar

Museo del Callejón

Museo del Farmacie

Casa del Libro
(Localización temporal)

C. Juan Antonio
Corretejas

Gambaro

Paseo de
Colón

Calle Marina

Calle Comercio

C. Tetuán

C. Tanca

C. Recinto Sur

Recinto
Oeste

C. San Francisco

Calle San Justo

Recinto Sur

Las Monjas

Calle Sol

Virtud

PUERTA DE
TIERRA

500 m

N

⊙ UNESCO World
Heritage Site

0

500 m

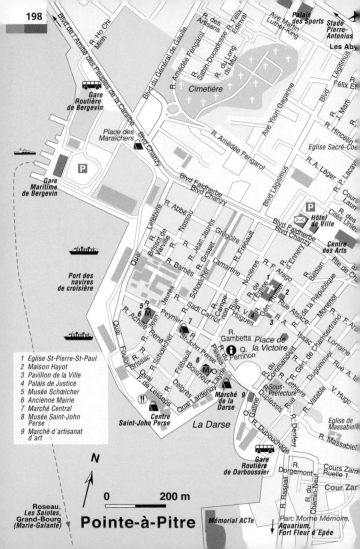

1 Eglise St-Pierre-St-Paul
2 Maison Hayot
3 Pavillon de la Ville
4 Palais de Justice
5 Musée Schœlcher
6 Ancienne Mairie
7 Marché Central
8 Musée Saint-John Perse
9 Marché d'artisanat d'art

N

0   200 m

Pointe-à-Pitre

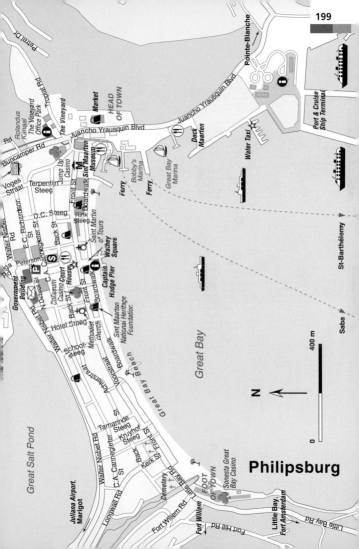

Philipsburg

Great Bay

Great Salt Pond

Pointe-Blanche

Port & Cruise Ship Terminal

St-Barthélemy

Saba

Juliana Airport, Marigot

Little Bay, Fort Amsterdam

Little Bay Rd

Fort Hill Rd

Fort Willem Rd

Fort Willem

Cemetery

Kerk St

Back St

Kruyhof Steeg

C.A. Cannegieter St

Tamarinde Steeg

Walter Nisbet Rd

Longwall Rd

FOOT OF TOWN

Sonesta Great Bay Casino

Great Bay Beach

Achterstraat

Voorstraat

School steeg

Methodist church

Hotel Steeg

Sint Maarten National Heritage Foundation

Boardwalk

Captain Hodge Pier

Wathey Square

Courthouse

Casino Court

Coliseum Casino

Peterson St

Government Building

Raga Rd

Walter Nisbet Rd

C.A. Cannegieter St

Back St

E.C. Richardson St

D.C. Steeg

Voges Straat

Terpentijn Steeg

Buncamper Rd

Rolandus Kanaal

Rolandus Rd

Petrel Dr

Tropial Rd

The Vineyard

The Vineyard Office Park

Market

HEAD OF TOWN

Juancho Yrausquin Blvd

Sint Maarten Museum

Jump Up Casino

Front St

Rink Steeg

Saint Martin of Tours

Bobby's Marina

Great Bay Marina

Dock Maarten

Water Taxi

Ferry

Ferry

N

0   400 m

Fort-de-Franc

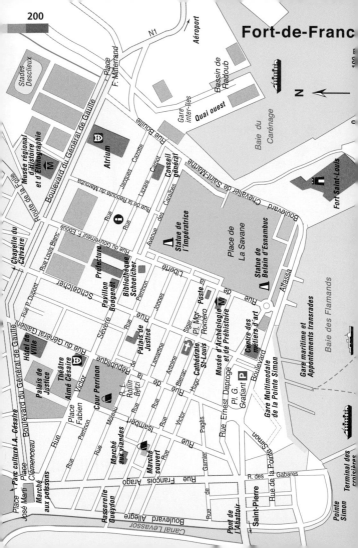

N1
Aéroport

Stades Desclieux

Place F. Mitterrand

Gare inter-îles

Quai ouest

Bassin de Radoub

Baie du Carénage

N

Musée régional d'Histoire et d'Ethnographie

Route de la Folie

Boulevard du Général de Gaulle

Rue de la Redoute du Matouba

Atrium

Rue Jacques Cazotte

Conseil général

Chevalier de Sainte-Marthe

Fort Saint-Louis

Chapelle du Calvaire

Rue du Gouverneur E. Éboué

Rue Lazare Carnot

Rue des Caraïbes

Statue de l'Impératrice

Place de La Savane

Rue Louis Blanc

Préfecture

Pavillon Bougenot

Bibliothèque Schoelcher

Rue Schoelcher

Rue Perrinon

Rue Bénion

Rue Jonnès

Avenue des Caraïbes

Liberté

Statue de Belain d'Esnambuc

Boulevard Alfassa

Baie des Flamands

Rue P. Dupont

Pl. Mgr Roméro

Poste

Rue Sévère

Palais de Justice

Rue Lamartine

Musée d'Archéologie et de Préhistoire

Centre des métiers d'art

Hôtel de Ville

Rue Blénac

Cathédrale St-Louis

Rue Antoine Siger

Boulevard

Gare maritime et Appontements transrades

Rue du Général Galliéni

Théâtre Aimé Césaire

Rue Victor Hugo

Cour Perrinon

Rue R. Rollin

Rue Betzi

Rue Ernest Deproge

Pl. G. Gratiant

P

Gare Multimodale de la Pointe Simon

Palais de Justice

Place Fabien

Rue Perrinon

Rue Moreau

Rue Isambert

Rue Victor Hugo

Rue Blénac

Rue Pagès

Rue de la Pointe Simon

Baie des Flamands

Parc culturel A. Césaire

Place José Marti

Place Clémenceau

Marché aux poissons

Rue du Général de Gaulle

Marché aux viandes

Marché couvert

Rue François Arago

Rue Garnier

R. des Gabares

Terminal des croisières

Passerelle Guydon

Boulevard Allègre

Pont de l'Abattoir

Saint-Pierre

Pointe Simon

Rue de la Pointe Simon

Canal Levassor

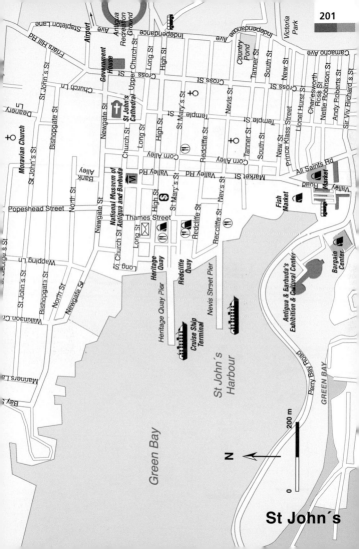

St John´s

Stapleton Lane
Friars Hill Rd
Airport
Antigua Ave
Antigua Recreation Ground
Independance Ave
Independance Ave
Victoria Park
Camacho Ave

Government House
Long St
High St
Cross St
Upper Church St
Country Pond
Tanner St
South St
New St
Charlesworth Ross St
Nellie Robinson St
Andy Roberts St
Sir Viv Richard's St

St John's St
Church Ln
Deanery Ln
Newgate St
St John's Cathedral
Church St
Long St
High St
St Mary's St
Temple St
Nevis St
Cross St
Tanner St
South St
New St
Lionel Hurst St
Prince Klass St

Moravian Church
Bishopgate St
Bank Alley
National Museum of Antigua and Barbuda
Corn Alley
Redcliffe St
Corn Alley
Market St
All Saints Rd
Valley Road

Popeshead Street
North St
Newgate St
Valley Rd
High St
St Mary's St
Valley Rd
Redcliffe St
Nevis St
Market
Fish Market

Wapping Ln
Bishopgate St
North St
Newgate St
Church St
Long St
Thames Street
High St
St Mary's St
Redcliffe St
Redcliffe St
Antigua & Barbuda's Exhibition & Cultural Center
Bargain Center

St John's St
St George's St
Wilkinson Cr
Heritage Quay
Redcliffe Quay
Nevis Street Pier
Green Bay

Mariner's La
Bay
Heritage Quay Pier
Cruise Ship Terminal
St John's Harbour
Perry Bay Rd

Green Bay

N

0   200 m

GREEN BAY

Caribbean
Sea

Canefield Aiport,
Portsmouth

Didier Ln

Leblanc Ln

Bowers Ln

STOCK
FARM

GOODWILL

Goodwill Rd

Bowers Ln

Watty Ln

Belfast Ln

Brandille Ln

Jolly Ln

Whyte Ln

Princess Margaret
Hospital

Terrel Ln

James Ln

Munro St

Eden
Ln

Charles Ave

Charles Ave

Federation Dr

Federation

Winston Ln

Winston Ln

Shop
Ln

Federation Dr

Lindo
Park

Dublin Ln

Grants Ln

Francis Ln

Churchill Ln

Rose St

Potter St

P H Dulwood Rd

Steber St

Church Ln

Federation Dr

Princess

Solomon

Jeffer's Ln

Murphy's Ln

Rose St

Franklyn Ln

POTTERS
VILLE

Goodwill Rd

Scotland Ln

Church

Canal
Ln

Eliot Ave

Steber St

Piveteau St

Potter St

St John's Ave

E C Loblack
Bridge

River

Roseau

River St

Government
Headquarters

Windsor
Park

MORNE
BRUCE

All Saints University

Queen Mary St

Hillsborough St

Kennedy Ave

Bath Rd

King George V St

Botanical
Gardens

Roseau New
Market

Hanover St

River St

Great George

Upper Ln

King's
Ave

Cork St

Virgin Ln

Bath Rd

City Council

Ship St

Hillsborough St

King's St

Upper Ln

Great Malborough St

Guadeloupe

Bay St

Long St

Kennedy

Drury Ln

Row Ln

Hodge's Ln

Old St

Cork St

Field St

King George V St

St Patrick's
Catholic
Cathedral

Queen Mary St

Ferry Terminal

N

Court-
house

Dominica Museum and
Old Market Square

Castle St

Methodist
Church

Jewel St

Cross St

Turkey St

Governor's
Residence

Roman Catholic
Cemetery

KING
HI...

Cruise Dock

Bay St

Church St

Anglican
Church

New Parliament
Building

High St

Gover St

Bath Rd

Anglican
Cemetery

Peebles
Park

Fort Young
Hotel

Public Library
and Museum

Cornwall St

Victoria St

Newtown
Savannah

0   200 m

Roseau

Martinique, St Lucia

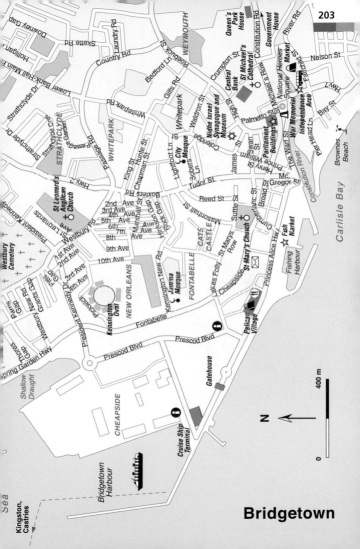

Downey Gap
Skette Rd
Holligan
Laundry Rd
Country Rd
Bedford St
Roebuck St
Lower Bank Hall Main Rd
Strathclyde Dr
Strathclyde Cr's Garden
STRATHCLYDE
Whitepark Rd
Passmore Rd
WHITEPARK
Hwy 3
St Leonard's Anglican Church
St Leonards Ave
President Kennedy
Westbury Cemetery
Paris Gap
The Gap
Westbund New Rd
Grants Gap
Lower Bank Hall Main Rd
Spring Garden Hwy
Thomas Gap
Shallow Draught
Sea
Kingston, Castries

WEYMOUTH
Queen's Park House
Government House
River Rd
Constitution Rd
Crumpton St
St Michael's Cathedral
Central Bank
National Heroes Square
Market
Nelson St
Fairchild St
Bay St
Browne's Beach
Palmetto St
St Michael's Row
War Memorial
Independence Arch
Parliament Buildings
The Wharf
Pier Head Ln
Constitution River
Carlisle Bay

Gills Rd
Whitepark
Waldron St
High St
Coleridge St
Nidhe Israel Synagogue and Museum
City Mosque
Sobers Ln
Lightfoot Ln
Tudor St
Reed St
James St
Swan St
Henry St
Prince William Henry St
McGregor St
Broad St
Cumberland St
Suttle St
Masonhall St
St Mary's Row
St Mary's Church
Princess Alice Hwy
Fish Market
Fishing Harbour

King St
Hunte St
Chapman St
Boxhers Rd
2nd Ave
3rd Ave
4th Ave
5th Ave
6th Ave
7th Ave
8th Ave
9th Ave
10th Ave
1st Ave
2nd Ave
3rd Ave
4th Ave
Westbury Rd
Marshall Ave
Hinson Gap
Rock Gap
GATS CASTLE
FONTABELLE
Jackes Ferry
Cheapside

President Kennedy Dr
Pickwick
Kensington Oval
NEW ORLEANS
Jumma Mosque
Kensington New Rd
Fontabelle
Fontabelle
Prescod Blvd
Prescod Blvd
Pelican Village
Gatehouse

CHEAPSIDE
Cruise Ship Terminal
Bridgetown Harbour

N
400 m
0

Bridgetown

Kingstown

Richmond Hill

E.T. Joshua Airport (3.2 km)
Indian Bay (5 km)
Villa Beach (6.5 km)

Sion Hill

Murray Rd

Sports Ground

Granby St

Sharp St

Tyrell Rd

South Rd

Grenadines

Wharf

Customs

Ferry Terminal

Courthouse

Halifax St

Egmont St

Middle St

Upper St

St

Cruise Ship Terminal

Bedford St

New Market

Hillsboro St

Upper Bay St

Deep Water Wharf

St Vincent Botanic Gardens (820 m)

St George's Cathedral

Grenville St

Fish Market

Fisheries Boat Dock

Kingstown Bay

Milton Cato Memorial Hospital

St Mary's Church

Methodist Church

Bay St

Grenville St

Lower Middle St

Lower Bay St

Grenville St

Fort Charlotte (2 km)

Cliff

N

300 m

0

Grenadines

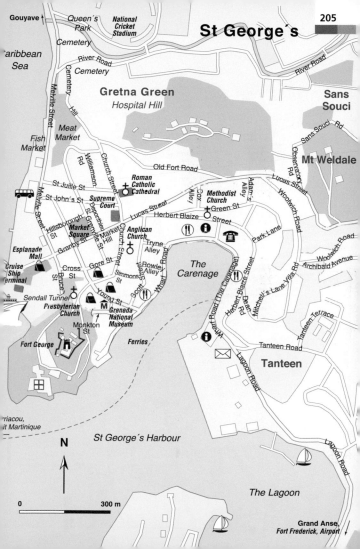

St George's

Gouyave

Queen's Park

National Cricket Stadium

Cemetery

Caribbean Sea

River Road

Cemetery

River Road

Gretna Green
Hospital Hill

Sans Souci

Melville Street

Hill

Cemetery

Meat Market

Sans Souci Rd

Mt Weldale

Observatory Rd

Fish Market

Williamson. Rd

Church Street

Old Fort Road

Lucas Street

St Juille St

Roman Catholic Cathedral

Methodist Church

Adam's Alley

Fox Alley

Woolwich Road

St John's St

Supreme Court

Depradine St

Grenville Hill

Lucas Street

Green St Street

Park Lane

Herbert Blaize

Hillsborough St

Market Square

Anglican Church

Market Street

Church Street

Woolwich Road

Granby St

Archibald Avenue

Esplanade Mall

Gore St.

Tryne Alley

The Carenage

Mitchell's Lane

Villa Rd

Cruise Ship Terminal

Bruce St.

Cross St.

Simmons St

Rowley Alley

Scott St

Wharf Road

Herbert Blaize Street

Dean Rd

Tanteen Terrace

Sendall Tunnel

Young St

Presbyterian Church

Wharf Road (The Carenage)

Tanteen Road

Monkton St

Grenada National Museum

Lagoon Road

Tanteen

Fort George

Ferries

Carriacou, Petit Martinique

St George's Harbour

N

0   300 m

The Lagoon

Grand Anse,
Fort Frederick, Airport

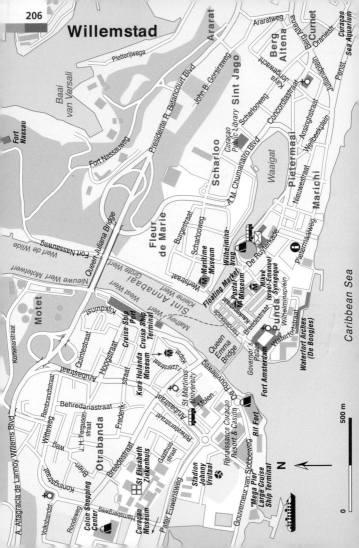

Anguilla 97–100
  Valley, The 97
Antigua 101–105
  Betty's Hope 105
  English Harbour 101
  Fig Tree Drive 105
  St John's 101, 201
Aruba 177–181
  Arikok National Park 181
  Balashi 181
  Noord 180
  Oranjestad 177
  Renaissance Island 180
  Rock Gardens 180
  San Nicolas 181
  Tunnel of Love 181
  West Coast 180
Bahamas 7–17
  Grand Bahama 12
    Freeport/Lucaya 12
  Nassau 7, 192
    Ardastra Gardens 11
    Cable Beach 11
    Clifton Heritage
      National Park 11
    Paradise Island 10
  Out Islands 15
    Abacos 15
    Andros 16
    Berry Islands 16
    Bimini 16
    Cat Island 16
    Crooked Island 16
    Eleuthera 15
    Exumas 16
    Great Inagua 16
    Long Island 16
    San Salvador 16
Barbados 144–149
  Atlantic Coast 148
  Bridgetown 144, 203
  Holetown 148
  Interior, The 149
  North, The 149
  Platinum Coast 148
Barbuda 105

Bonaire 182–185
  Flamingo Sanctuary
    183
  Kralendijk 182
  Lac Bay 183
  Rincón 183
  Washington Slagbaai
    National Park 182
British Virgin Islands
    69–74
  Anegada 73
  Jost Van Dyke 73
  Norman Island 73
  Peter Island 73
  Salt Island 73
  Tortola 69
  Virgin Gorda 72
Caicos Islands 23
Cayman Islands 27–33
  Cayman Brac 32
  Grand Cayman 27
  Little Cayman 32
Curaçao 186–190
  Chobolobo 190
  Christoffel Nat. Park 190
  Hato Caves 190
  Ostrich Farm 190
  Willemstad 186, 206
Desirade, La Guadeloupe
Dominica 132–137
  East Coast, The 137
  Interior, The 133
  Morne Trois Pitons
    National Park 133
  Roseau 132, 202
  West Coast, The 136
Dominican Republic 49–55
  Boca Chica 54
  Isla Catalina 54
  – Saona 54
  La Romana 54, 195
  Peninsula de la
    Samaná, 54
  San Pedro de Macorís 54
  Santo Domingo 49, 196
    Zona Colonial 49

French Antilles 106–126
  Guadeloupe 111
  Martinique 119
  Saint-Barthélemy 109
  Saint-Martin 106
Grenada 158–162
  Carriacou 162
  East Coast 161
  Grand-Etang Road 162
  Northern Tip 161
  Petit Martinique 162
  St George's 158, 205
  West Coast 161
Grenadines 155–157
  Bequia 155
  Canouan 156
  Mayreau 157
  Mustique 156
  Palm 157
  Petit St Vincent 157
  Tobago Cays 156
  Union 157
Guadeloupe 111–118
  Basse-Terre 115
  Grande-Terre 111
  La Désirade 117
  Les Saintes 118
  Marie-Galante 117
  Pointe-à-Pitre 111, 198
  Soufrière, La 116
Jamaica 35–47
  Blue Mountains 39
  Cockpit Country 46
  Discovery Bay 44
  Dunn's River Falls 43
  Falmouth 44
  Kingston 35
    Lime Cay 39
    Port Royal 37
  Montego Bay 45, 194
  Negril 46
  Ocho Rios 42
  Oracabessa 42
  Port Antonio 41
  Port Maria 42
  Runaway Bay 44

Spanish Town 39
St Ann's Bay 43
Marie-Galante Guadeloupe
Martinique 119–125
  Atlantic Coast 123
  Fort-de-France 119, 200
  Northern Beaches 122
  Route de la Trace 123
  West Coast 120
Montserrat 96
Nevis 131
Puerto Rico 57–67
  **Centro Ceremonial
  – Indígena Caguana** 66
  – Indígena de Tibes 65
  El Yunque 63
  Fajardo 63
  Isla Mona 65
  Luquillo 63
  Mayagüez 65
  Ponce 63
  Rincón 65
  Río Camuy 66
  San Germán 65
  San Juan 57
    Old Town 57, 197
    Metropolitan Area 61
Saba 87–89
  Saba Marine Park 89
Saint-Barthélemy 109
Saint-Martin (FR) 106
  Marigot 106
Saintes, Les Guadeloupe
St Croix US Virgin Islands
St John US Virgin Islands
St Kitts 127–131
  Basseterre 127
  Brimstone Hill Fort 130
  Dieppe Bay Town 131
  Frigate Bay 131
  Scenic Railway 130
St Lucia 138–143
  Castries 138
  Vieux Fort to Dennery 143
  North, The 139
  Pigeon Island 139

Soufrière 142
South, The 142
St Thomas 75–80
  Brewer's Bay 79
  Charlotte Amalie 75
  Coral World Ocean P. 80
  Drake's Seat 79
  Frenchtown 79
  Hassel Island 78
  Mountain Top 79
St Vincent 150–154
  Atlantic Coast 154
  Caribbean Coast 152
  Kingstown 150, 204
  La Soufrière 154
  South, The 153
Sint Maarten (NL) 93
  Philipsburg 93, 199
**Statia (Sint
  Eustatius)** 89
  Hikes 90
  Oranjestad 89
Tobago 171–174
  Atlantic Coast 173
  Caribbean Coast 172
  Scarborough 171
  Southwest 171
Trinidad 165–170
  **Asa Wright Nature
  Centre** 170
  Caroni Swamp 170
  Chaguaramas 169
  Maracas–St Joseph 170
  Port of Spain 165
  North Coast 170
  West Coast 170
Turks and Caicos 19–24
  Grand Turk 19
    Cockburn Town 19
  Pine Cay 24
  Providenciales 24
US Virgin Islands 75–85
  Buck Island 83
  St Croix 81
  St John 80
  St Thomas 75

Editors
Polly Thomas

Concept
Karin Palazzolo

Layout
Luc Malherbe
Matias Jolliet

Photo credits
p. 1: hemis.fr/Gardel;
p. 2: istockphoto.com/Saspartout
  (lime);
  istockphoto.com/Pruter
  (starfish);
  istockphoto.com/Eichenberge
  (lizard);
  fotolia.com/Fouquin
  (bougainvillaea)

Maps
JPM Publications
Mathieu Germay

Copyright © 2015, 2012
JPM Publications S.A.
12, avenue William-Fraisse,
1006 Lausanne, Switzerland
information@jpmguides.com
http://www.jpmguides.com/

Printed in Germany
14997.00.18299
Edition 2016